ETHIOPIA

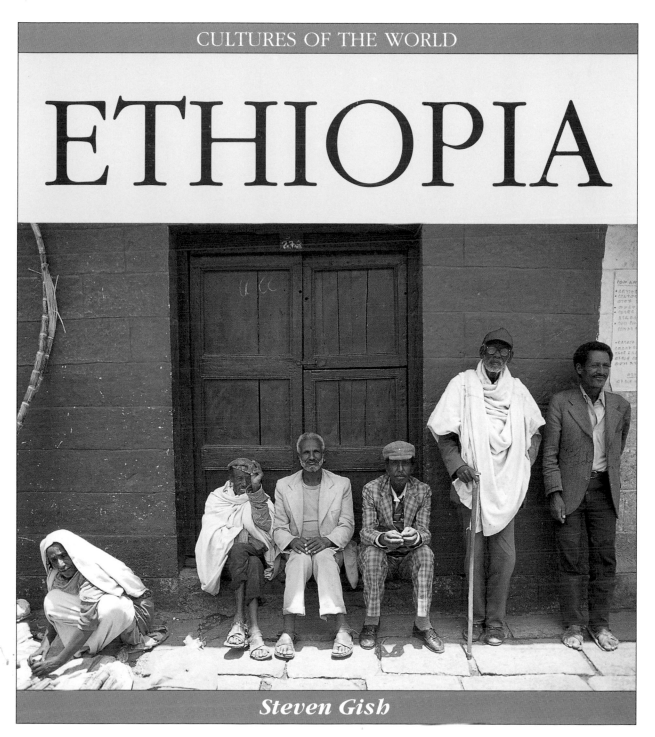

Steven Gish

MARSHALL CAVENDISH
New York • London • Sydney

Reference edition published 1997 by
Marshall Cavendish Corporation
99 White Plains Road
Tarrytown
New York 10591

© Times Editions Pte Ltd 1996

Originated and designed by
Times Books International, an imprint of
Times Editions Pte Ltd

Printed in Singapore

Library of Congress Cataloging-in-Publication Data:
Gish, Steven, 1963-
    Ethiopia / Steven Gish.
      p. cm.—(Cultures Of The World)
    Includes bibliographical references and index.
    Summary: Introduces the geography, history, government,
economy, culture, daily life, and people of the country known
as "the roof of Africa."
    ISBN 0-7614-0276-4 (lib. bdg.)
    1. Ethiopia—Juvenile literature. [1. Ethiopia.] I. Title.
II. Series.
DT373.G48 1996
963—dc20   95–44861
               CIP
               AC

INTRODUCTION

ETHIOPIA IS A LAND OF incredible diversity. It is home to more than 100 different ethnic groups, 70 languages, and adherents of four major religions. Among the most mountainous countries in Africa, Ethiopia's landscape includes jagged peaks, grasslands and forests, deep valleys, lakes and waterfalls, and stretches of desert.

This rugged land has a rich, ancient history. In fact, Ethiopia may be the place where human history began more than four million years ago. Up until 1974, Ethiopia was governed by one of the world's oldest monarchies. Contemporary Ethiopia is a country in transition. Warfare and famine cost the lives of hundreds of thousands of Ethiopians in the 1980s. In 1991, the military government was toppled by forces that pledged to undertake democratic reforms. Trying to rebuild their nation amid so much ethnic, linguistic, and cultural diversity is the main challenge facing Ethiopians today.

CONTENTS

Two girls stand in the doorway of their home. Poverty plagues the majority of Ethiopians.

CONTENTS

Surma women wear lip plugs to improve their looks.

5

GEOGRAPHY

ETHIOPIA IS LOCATED in the "Horn of Africa," that part of the African continent that juts out into the Indian Ocean and lies just to the south of the Arabian Peninsula. Directly to the north of Ethiopia lies Eritrea, which gained its independence from Ethiopia in 1993. Bordering Ethiopia to the east is Djibouti; to the south and east, Somalia; to the south, Kenya; and to the west, Sudan. Ethiopia lies entirely between the equator and the tropic of Cancer. Its territory spans 437,600 square miles (1,133,380 square kilometers), making it nearly three times larger than California.

Ethiopia is one of the most mountainous countries in Africa. It contains two vast highland regions separated by the Great Rift Valley, a vast low-lying area that divides the country roughly in half. Elevations in both highland regions often measure 7,500 feet (2,300 meters) and higher. Ethiopia's rugged terrain makes regional transportation and communication difficult, but it has also historically protected the country from invaders.

Another key feature of Ethiopia's geography is the lack of reliable rainfall in several parts of the country. Precipitation is particularly scant in low-lying areas such as the Rift Valley, the Ogaden region in the southeast, and the Denakil Depression in the northeast. Droughts in these areas caused major famines in both 1973 and 1984 and claimed thousands of lives. Similar dry spells can be expected to torment the Ethiopian people in the future.

Above and left: **Ethiopia is situated in an area of intense geological activity, as evidenced by the many small volcanoes, hot springs, and gorges that punctuate its landscape. Several volcanoes lie in the Denakil Depression alone; seismic faults there also cause periodic earthquakes.**

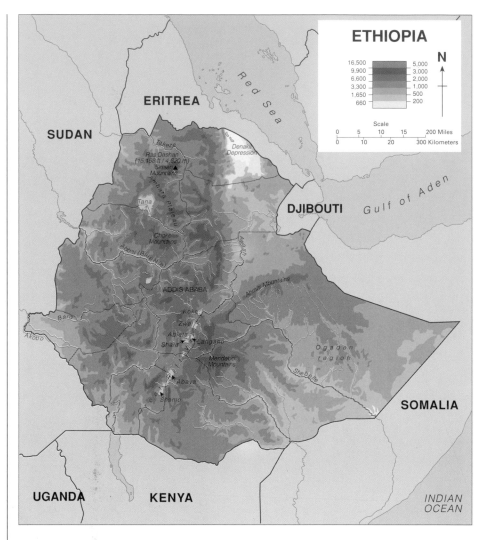

Ras Dashan Peak, located in the Simien Mountains, is the highest point in Ethiopia, soaring to 15,158 feet (4,620 meters).

PEAKS AND VALLEYS

Elevation is the single most important factor affecting Ethiopia's geography. It determines the climate, vegetation, soil composition, and settlement patterns of every region in the country.

Because of its mountainous terrain, Ethiopia is sometimes referred to as "the roof of Africa." Its two major highland regions dominate the western and south central portions of the country. Rising to the west of the Great Rift Valley is the Amhara Plateau, home to the Simien and Choke mountain ranges. These western highlands generally range in elevation from 7,800 to 12,000 feet (2,400–3,700 meters) above sea level. The Somali Plateau lies to the east of the Rift Valley and contains the Ahmar and Mendebo mountains. Several peaks in the Mendebo mountains rise above 13,000 feet (3,950 meters).

Valleys, deserts, and grasslands also contribute to the country's varied landscape. The Great Rift Valley cuts through much of east Africa and extends all the way to Mozambique in southern Africa. In Ethiopia the Rift Valley ranges from 25 to 40 miles wide (40–65 kilometers). The northern portion of the valley contains the Denakil Depression, a desert area that lies 380 feet (116 meters) below sea level. The valley's southwestern portion is dotted by a chain of freshwater and salt lakes.

The Blue Nile flows south from Lake Tana and is the country's longest river, flowing for 850 miles (1,367 kilometers) into neighboring Sudan.

LAKES AND RIVERS

The chain of lakes in the Great Rift Valley includes lakes Abaya, Abiata, Koka, Langano, Shala, Shamo, and Zwai. Ethiopia's largest lake is Lake Tana, which lies in the northern part of the country. This freshwater lake is the source of the Blue Nile River.

The Blue Nile is known to many Ethiopians as the Abbai River. Other smaller rivers in Ethiopia include the Awash, Baro, Shebeile, and Tekeze. The government has built dams on the Awash River to generate hydroelectric power and to provide irrigation for commercial farms. Most of Ethiopia's rivers originate in highland areas and flow outward through deep gorges. This has created a series of rapids and waterfalls that, though scenic, make navigation on the rivers virtually impossible. Of all of Ethiopia's rivers, only the Baro is fully navigable.

A MULTITUDE OF CLIMATES

The climate in Ethiopia is determined to a large extent by elevation, and thus varies a great deal from one region to the next. The highlands generally receive at least 39 inches (99 centimeters) of rainfall per year and experience moderate to cool temperatures. The hospitable climate of the highland regions helps explain why they are home to the majority of Ethiopia's population. Situated in the highlands is Addis Ababa, Ethiopia's capital and largest city. Addis Ababa's average temperature is 59°F (15°C); its average annual rainfall totals 49 inches (124 centimeters).

The Ethiopian lowlands are much drier than the highlands and usually receive less than 19.5 inches (50 centimeters) of rain per year. These areas are located chiefly in the north-central and eastern portions of the country and constitute the hottest parts of Ethiopia. Population density in the lowlands is significantly lower than it is on the plateaus.

Precipitation is influenced by both elevation and season. Ethiopia receives most of its precipitation during the rainy season, which lasts from June to September. Southwestern Ethiopia is the most well-watered part of the country and receives an average of 56 inches (140 centimeters) of rainfall per year. Rainfall is scant in the Great Rift Valley and the Ogaden region. Drier still is the

ETHIOPIA'S CLIMATIC ZONES

1. Alpine (*kur,* "kuhr")

Location: Ethiopia's highest elevations.

Elevation: Over 10,800 feet (3,300 meters).

Temperatures: Below 50°F (10°C).

Features of interest: Regular frost; snow on highest mountain peaks. Unsuitable for agriculture.

2. Cool zone (*dega,* "DEH-ga")

Location: Chiefly northwestern (Amhara) plateau.

Elevation: 7,500–10,800 feet (2,300–3,300 meters).

Temperatures: 34°F–61°F (1°C–16°C).

Features of interest: Warmest months are March-May. Light frost is common at night in the higher elevations.

3. Temperate zone (*weina dega,* "WAY-nuh DEH-ga")

Location: Lower areas of Amhara and Somali plateaus.

Elevation: 4,900–7,500 feet (1,500–2,300 meters).

Temperatures: 59°F–72°F (15°C–22°C).

4. Hot zone (*kolla,* "KOH-la")

Location: Eastern Ogaden, valleys of the Blue Nile and Tekeze rivers, and areas along Kenyan and Sudanese borders.

Elevation: 1,600–4,900 feet (500–1,500 meters).

Temperatures: Average daytime temperature is 81°F (27°C).

Features of interest: The river valleys receive more rainfall than do the border areas.

5. Semidesert (*bereha,* "ber-eh-HAH")

Location: Denakil Depression and other scattered, low-lying regions of Ethiopia.

Elevation: Below 1,600 feet (500 meters).

Temperatures: 86°F–120°F (30°C–49°C).

Features of interest: Arid; unsuitable for agriculture.

The rainy season is regarded as winter, even though it falls during the summer months, because cloud cover and rains reduce the temperature. The high plateau often gets heavy hailstorms during the rainy season.

Denakil Depression, which receives only a few inches of precipitation annually. In bad years there is no rain at all. The Ethiopian drought of 1984 claimed the lives of over 300,000 people and put eight million more on the brink of starvation. Pictures of malnourished Ethiopian children and crowded refugee camps were broadcast all over the world and triggered a massive international relief effort.

VEGETATION

The amount of rainfall (or lack thereof) in Ethiopia's various regions greatly affects the variety and quantity of plant life. In the driest areas, only occasional bushes and thorn scrub are found. In areas classified as semi-arid, grasslands are common, as are Acacia trees and sansevieria (snake plants). The cooler and wetter highlands are home to eucalyptus and yellowwood trees and juniper. Southwestern Ethiopia's combination of low elevation and high rainfall has produced rainforests thick with trees, ferns, and undergrowth. Some of Ethiopia's world-famous coffee grows wild in these southwestern rainforests.

ANIMAL LIFE

Ethiopia is home to an extraordinarily wide range of mammals, reptiles, fish, and birds. Roaming the grasslands are antelope, elephants, gazelle, giraffes, hyenas, jackals, leopards, lions, rhinos, and zebras. Baboons and colobus monkeys are commonly found in the forested areas. Unique to Ethiopia is the Walia ibex, a rare species of mountain goat that is found in the Simien Mountains. The country's lakes and rivers host crocodiles, hippos, and various other reptiles and species of fish. The Great Rift Valley is known for its bird life, which includes eagles, flamingos, and hawks. Other birds native to Ethiopia include the egret, hornbill, ibis, ostrich, pelican, stork, and vulture.

Geladas, similar to baboons, inhabit the mountains of southern Ethiopia, living on the cliffs of rocky ravines.

ENVIRONMENTAL CONCERNS

Two major problems confronting the Ethiopian landscape are deforestation and desertification. In 1900, approximately 30 percent of Ethiopia was covered by forest, but by the mid-1980s, this figure had fallen to less than 3 percent. Forests have been cleared to make room for more farmland, but overgrazing in many areas has led to a loss of ground cover and erosion. The gradual spread of the desert has shrunk the amount of land suitable for agriculture. Desertification is particularly severe in northern Ethiopia, where the risk of famine has risen sharply in recent years. Many Ethiopians farm in areas that have marginal or unreliable rainfall, thus exacerbating potential drought and famine conditions.

The environmental news is not all negative, however. Ethiopia contains deposits of gold and platinum, which form the basis of a small mining industry. The country also contains other mineral resources that are largely untapped, such as copper, lead, magnesium, and iron. Deposits of clay, limestone, salt, and oil have been uncovered as well.

Shepherds stop for water at an oasis in the Denakil Desert. The loss of grazing land to desert is a contributing factor to Ethiopia's recurring famines.

A RICH URBAN HERITAGE

Although only 12 percent of Ethiopians live in urban areas, the cities they inhabit have long histories and compelling points of interest. Addis Ababa, the capital, has been described as a "cultural jigsaw puzzle" because of its rich mixture of peoples and lifestyles. It is also one of the largest inland cities in Africa. According to the last official census (conducted in 1984) Addis Ababa's population was 1,412,577; a government estimate in 1993 put the figure at 2,200,186. The city is situated in the highlands at an altitude of 8,000 feet (2,440 meters) and enjoys a temperate climate.

Besides serving as Ethiopia's capital, Addis Ababa is also an important diplomatic center for the African continent. It is home to approximately 80 foreign embassies and hosts international agencies such as the World Health Organization (WHO) and the United Nations International Children's Emergency Fund (UNICEF). The city also serves as the headquarters for the Organization of African Unity (OAU).

Ethiopia's second largest city is Dire Dawa, which had a population of 173,588 according to a 1993 estimate. Dire Dawa lies between Addis Ababa and the coast and serves as an important rail terminus. In addition to Addis Ababa and Dire Dawa, Ethiopia has seven cities with over 100,000 residents: Harer, Gondar, Nazret, Mekele, Jima, Dese, and Bahir Dar.

ADDIS ABABA: HISTORY AND POINTS OF INTEREST

Modern Addis Ababa began to take shape in 1889, when the Ethiopian monarch Menelik II started building a palace near the ruins of the 16th-century capital at Entoto. Menelik's Queen Taytu marveled at the flowering mimosa trees in the area, and thus the town was named Addis Ababa, meaning "new flower." It officially became Ethiopia's capital in 1896. Other important dates for Addis Ababa are 1958, when the city became the first headquarters of the United Nations Economic Commission for Africa, and 1963, when it hosted the African Heads of State Conference at which the OAU Charter was signed.

Among the many points of interest in Addis Ababa, two in particular stand out. One is the Giorgis Cathedral, built in 1896 to commemorate Ethiopia's victory over the Italians at the Battle of Adwa.

Giorgis Cathedral features impressive stained glass created by Ethiopian artist Afewerk Tekle. Another urban wonder is the "Merkato," one of Africa's largest open-air markets. Here a dazzling array of goods are displayed for sale, including vegetables, spices, clothing, and jewelry. Because it draws Ethiopians from far beyond the capital, the Merkato has been described as a melting pot for the country's different languages and cultures.

Two cities of particular historical significance are Axum and Gondar. Axum, located in northern Ethiopia near the Eritrean border, was the capital of ancient Ethiopia. Two thousand years ago this holy city was on a par with the great urban centers of Nubia, Egypt, and Greece. Axum is home to St. Mary of Zion Church, built in the 16th and 17th centuries and considered to be the holiest shrine in Ethiopia. Axum is also noted for huge granite sculptures known as obelisks, some of which are over 75 feet (23 meters) tall. Gondar, located just north of Lake Tana, served as the Ethiopian capital between 1632 and 1868. Today some of its surviving castles are used as government office buildings.

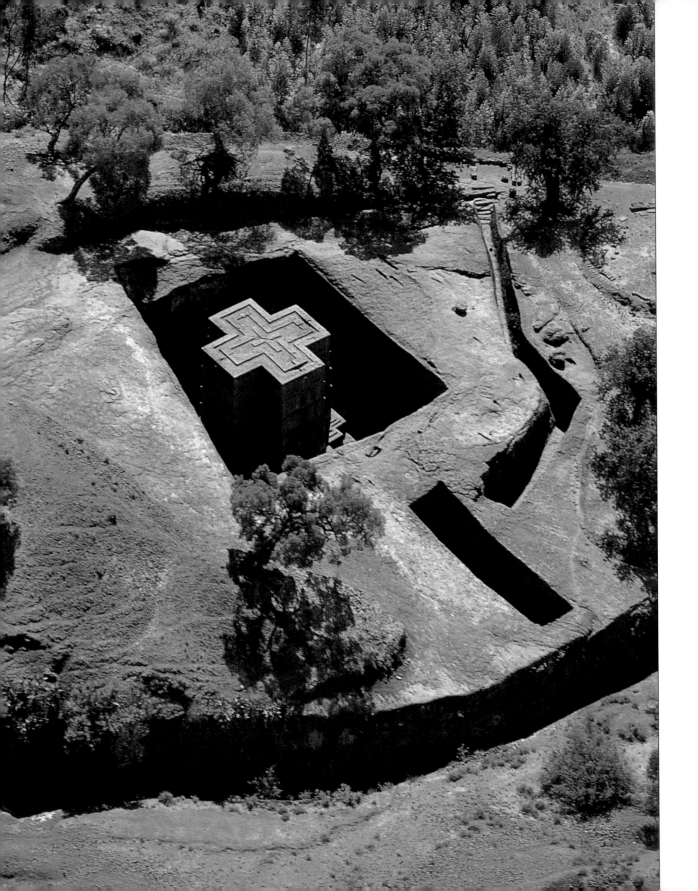

HISTORY

THERE IS MUCH that makes the history of Ethiopia unique. First and perhaps most significant, Ethiopia was home to the earliest human ancestors. A team of anthropologists has recently discovered skeletal remains of human-like beings that date back over four million years. Second, Ethiopia embraced an early form of Christianity over 1,000 years before European missionaries spread this religion throughout the rest of Africa. Third, Ethiopia was one of only two African countries to remain independent during the era of European colonization beginning in the late 19th century. (The other country was Liberia in West Africa.) Finally, Ethiopia was involved in modern Africa's longest war, the Eritrean conflict, which lasted from 1962 to 1991.

EARLY HUMAN ANCESTORS

In November 1994, Yohannes Haile Selassie, an Ethiopian scientist trained in the United States, made a once-in-a-lifetime discovery. While examining a hillside near Aramis on Ethiopia's Awash River, the researcher uncovered a group of human-like hand bones that were approximately 4.4 million years old. Soon other anthropologists working in the area found additional bones from the same creature and reconstructed almost the entire skeleton. In January 1995, the scientists announced their discovery to the world. They had found remnants of the extinct species *Australopithecus ramidus*, the world's oldest-known human ancestor.

Archaeological evidence found in Ethiopia attests to the early hominid activity in the region. This evidence includes stone hand tools, sharp cutting instruments, and drawings in limestone caves near Dire Dawa. By approximately 5000 B.C., hunters and gatherers had established communities on the Ethiopian highlands. Grain cultivation and animal husbandry appeared in the northwest highlands sometime before 2000 B.C.

Skeletal remains from the second-oldest human ancestor were also found in Ethiopia. This skeleton, known as "Lucy," was discovered in 1974 and is approximately 3.1 million years old. Ethiopians call the Lucy skeleton "Dinkenesh," meaning "she is wonderful."

Opposite: **King Lalibela, who ruled from approximately 1185 to 1225, authorized the construction of 11 churches carved out of solid rock. They remain to this day in the town that bears his name.**

The primary language of the Axumite kingdom was Ge'ez, a vernacular that gave rise to Amharic in the Middle Ages.

THE KINGDOM OF AXUM

Modern Ethiopia traces its origins to the great kingdom of Axum, which was one of Africa's most important cultural and trading centers during the first millennium A.D. Migrants from southern Arabia laid the foundations of the kingdom by bringing their language and stone-building traditions to the northeastern African coast beginning around 1000 B.C.

The Axumite kingdom began to take shape in the first centuries A.D. in the north and central portions of present-day Ethiopia. The kingdom became a thriving trading center in which merchants exchanged gold and ivory for cloth, glassware, tools, and other materials.

Christianity became the state religion of the Axumite kingdom during King Ezanas's rule in the 4th century. The establishment of the Ethiopian Orthodox Church—heavily influenced by the Coptic Church in Egypt—

Merchants from Axum traded not only in Axum, but with inhabitants of what is now Sudan, the Nile River valley, the Red Sea coast, southern Arabia, and the eastern Mediterranean. Testifying to Axum's wealth were the many temples, castles, and obelisks constructed in this era, some of which survive to this day.

THE ORIGINS OF THE ETHIOPIAN MONARCHY

According to Harold Marcus, a prominent historian of Ethiopia, many of the legends surrounding the Ethiopian ruling dynasty originated in the 14th century. In this period, six Tigrayan scribes proclaimed that the country's monarchy was descended from the Queen of Sheba and King Solomon, in order to infuse the monarchy with a glorious past and create a proud heritage for the Ethiopian kingdom. Whether or not the scribes' proclamation was completely true puzzles historians to this day.

The legend claims that in the 10th century B.C., the Queen of Sheba visited King Solomon in Jerusalem, who became her mentor in the art of royal statecraft. The queen eventually converted to Judaism and became romantically involved with King Solomon. She then returned to Ethiopia and bore a son, Menelik I, who was declared king of that country by his father, King Solomon.

After Menelik's death, those claiming to be his descendants ruled the kingdom of Axum for centuries. The Zagwe dynasty temporarily interrupted the "Solomonic" line, but by the 13th century, a new king claiming to be one of Menelik's descendants gained the throne. Thus the Solomonic dynasty was restored, even though some of Menelik's successors may not have been his direct descendants. The dynasty would continue to rule Ethiopia until Emperor Haile Selassie's ouster in 1974.

would entrench the Christian tradition in Ethiopia for centuries to come. But other religious traditions also gained a foothold in Ethiopia. Judaism began spreading in the region in the early sixth century, and Islam started to gain converts two centuries later along the coast. The rise of Islam in the 10th and 11th centuries led to the decline of Axum, as Christians retreated to the highlands and lost their preeminence in the kingdom's outlying regions.

THE ZAGWE DYNASTY

The Zagwe dynasty, which ruled Ethiopia in the 12th and 13th centuries, temporarily broke the Solomonic hold on the Ethiopian monarchy. This period is seen as an era of great artistic achievement, during which impressive rock churches were carved and dedicated to the glory of God.

NEW CONTACTS AND CONFLICTS

The Solomonic dynasty was restored around 1270 A.D. During the next two centuries, the new regime consolidated its authority and encouraged the spread of the Amharic language and Orthodox Christianity throughout the Ethiopian highlands.

By the late 15th century, however, incursions by outsiders threatened to destabilize the established order. In the late 1400s, a Portuguese contingent traveled to Ethiopia in hopes of finding Christian allies to help them curb the growing Islamic presence in the region. When Muslims launched an attack against Ethiopia in 1527, the Ethiopians appealed to the Portuguese for aid. The combined Ethiopian-Portuguese forces turned back the Muslim invaders. In this era, the Ethiopians still viewed Europeans as allies, despite rebuffing Portuguese attempts to spread Roman Catholicism in their country.

Ethiopian contacts with Europe became steadily more difficult until Menelik II finally defeated the Italians and secured Ethiopia's independence.

Contacts between Ethiopia and Europe were relatively infrequent between the mid-17th and late 18th centuries. The situation changed dramatically in the 19th century, however. In this era, Italy, Britain, and France cast their eyes on Ethiopia. Three Ethiopian emperors stood in the way of the European colonial advance: Tewodros II (ruled 1855–1868),

Yohannis IV (1872–1889), and Menelik II (1889–1913). During the Napier expedition of 1867–68, a British force of 3,000 troops was sent to Ethiopia to secure the release of British officials held by Emperor Tewodros. As the British troops advanced, Tewodros committed suicide to avoid capture. The British soon withdrew from Ethiopia, but the Italians seemed more anxious to stay. They acquired the ports of Aseb in 1869 and Massawa in 1885 before being turned back by Ethiopian forces.

MENELIK II

Emperor Menelik II faced still greater threats to Ethiopia's sovereignty. Shortly after he came to power in 1889, Menelik signed a treaty allowing the Italians to occupy Asmara, but renounced it in 1893 when Italy sought to extend its authority to Ethiopia as a whole. When the Italians began moving southward into Ethiopian territory, Menelik distributed weapons obtained from France and Russia, constructed a national army from Ethiopia's diverse ethnic groups, and readied his troops for battle. On March 1, 1896, the Ethiopian army confronted the Italians at the battle of Adwa, and scored a decisive victory. The peace treaty signed later that year preserved Ethiopia's independence during the height of the European "scramble for Africa." The kingdom emerged from its victory with considerable prestige, both in Africa and Europe.

An Ethiopian painting shows the Battle of Adwa. This Ethiopian victory secured Ethiopia's independence. Historians Richard Pankhurst and John Markakis sum up this period: "For 25 years Ethiopia had maintained its independence against European encroachments, through the skill of Menelik and the military courage of his people. . . and through the utilization of the mutual jealousies of the rival European powers."

THE ERA OF HAILE SELASSIE

Haile Selassie I ruled Ethiopia between 1930 and 1974, and is considered one of 20th-century Africa's most important leaders. During Haile Selassie's reign, Ethiopia began to modernize its political and economic system, despite facing threats of famine, foreign occupation, and ethnic division.

Haile Selassie's first challenge was to preserve Ethiopian independence in the face of renewed Italian aggression. In October 1935, Italy invaded Ethiopia in an attempt to avenge its loss at Adwa 39 years earlier. Italian troops entered Addis Ababa on May 5, 1936, and formally annexed Ethiopia four days later. The emperor went into exile in Britain and appealed to the League of Nations to take strong action against the Italians, but initially little was done. Fortunately for Ethiopia, the Italian occupation did not last. With the help of the British, Haile Selassie organized an Ethiopian resistance force in neighboring Sudan and led an invasion into Ethiopia in January 1941. The Emperor's troops reentered Addis Ababa on May 5, 1941, five years to the day after the Italian conquest. Following Italy's surrender on May 20, 1941, Haile Selassie was reestablished as emperor.

The Era of Haile Selassie

Haile Selassie initiated important reforms in Ethiopia between the 1940s and 1960s. He encouraged the development of a secular educational system; attracted Western economic and technical assistance; approved a new constitution (1955), which provided for parliamentary elections; curbed the power of the aristocracy and church; and declared Amharic the official language of Ethiopia. He also played an active role in the establishment of the Organization of African Unity (OAU), which first met in Addis Ababa in 1963. Subsequently the city became the site of the OAU's headquarters.

Internal pressures posed serious problems for Haile Selassie's government, particularly from the 1960s onward. Eritreans began their long armed struggle against Ethiopian rule in 1962. In the late 1960s and early 1970s, students clashed with police during demonstrations for Eritrean independence and for land and educational reform. To make matters worse, a major famine broke out in the Tigray and Welo provinces in 1972–74, causing the deaths of approximately 200,000 Ethiopians. By 1974, groups of students, workers, and soldiers were demanding the dismissal of Haile Selassie's cabinet. The emperor, then aged 82, was unable to stem the rising tide of discontent. On September 12, 1974, a group of army officers deposed Haile Selassie and set up a new military government. The 3,000-year-old Ethiopian monarchy had finally come to an end.

Haile Selassie died in Ethiopia in August 1975 while under house arrest. He was allegedly killed by backers of the new military government.

The OAU headquarters in Addis Ababa.

THE STRUGGLE FOR ERITREA

Tensions between Ethiopia and Eritrea began shortly after World War II. Following the war, the United Nations nullified Italian control over Eritrea and placed it under the Ethiopian crown as an autonomous territory. In 1962, Haile Selassie annexed Eritrea so that Ethiopia could gain full control over the ports of Massawa and Aseb. Eritreans quickly established the Eritrean Liberation Front to spearhead their bid for independence. Few realized that 30 years of bitter struggle lay ahead.

After eight years of sporadic guerilla warfare, a new Marxist group gained control over the rebel forces in Eritrea: the Eritrean People's Liberation Front (EPLF). The fighting in Eritrea escalated into a full-scale conventional war in 1975. In 1978, the Ethiopian army forced the Eritrean rebels from the cities to the countryside, where the war continued. The tide turned in favor of the Eritreans in the late 1980s. In 1988, the EPLF captured the Ethiopian army headquarters at Af Abed; two years later the EPLF gained control over Massawa. In 1991, the EPLF occupied Aseb and Asmara, and was powerful enough to establish a provisional government in Eritrea.

The 1991 collapse of the Mengistu government in Addis Ababa effectively ended Ethiopian control over Eritrea. In April 1993, 99.8% of Eritreans voted in favor of independence in a special referendum held in the territory. On May 25, 1993, Eritrea officially became an independent nation. EPLF leader Issayas Afewerki was elected president the following month. Although some Ethiopians still oppose Eritrean independence, relations between the new governments in Asmara and Addis Ababa have generally been good.

ETHIOPIA UNDER MILITARY RULE, 1974–1991

With the overthrow of Haile Selassie, the Ethiopian monarchy was abolished and replaced by a military regime, and the country's economic orientation shifted from capitalism to Marxism. The new regime that took power in mid-1974 was known as the *Derg* ("durg"), an Amharic word meaning "committee." The Derg, which was composed of 120 military officers, was led by an Eritrean general, Aman Andom. During its first few months, the regime instituted press censorship, limited civil rights, and executed 60 former imperial officials. Next the regime suspended the constitution and dissolved parliament.

In December 1974, the government announced the creation of a one-party state and began to restructure the Ethiopian economy along socialist lines. Officials drew up plans for collective farms, confiscated private property, and nationalized many foreign-owned corporations. Many of those who opposed the regime—including students, church leaders, and members of the former government—were imprisoned, forced into exile, or killed.

The rise of Lt. Colonel Mengistu Haile Mariam ushered in even more violence. The military government had launched a major new effort to wipe out its opponents in 1976, but Mengistu intensified the campaign when he came to power in 1977. During the Red Terror of 1976–78, over 100,000 Ethiopians are believed to have been killed by the military authorities. In May 1977, the government executed 500 students. Ethiopians who survived the fearful days and nights of the Red Terror recall seeing new victims of the government's campaign of terror almost every day.

Mengistu Haile Mariam presided over the Red Terror of 1976–78. The state-run radio would broadcast the names of those who had just been executed and label the victims as "anti-revolutionaries," "reactionaries," or "enemies of the state."

The Mengistu government received significant economic and military assistance from the Soviet Union beginning in the late 1970s, and thus initially maintained a firm grip on power. But escalating crises at home began to cripple the regime by the 1980s. Insurgencies in Eritrea, Tigray, and the Ogaden challenged the Ethiopian military machine more seriously than ever before. In 1983, a massive famine broke out in Ethiopia, claiming the lives of at least 300,000 people by 1985. Although a major international relief effort was launched to aid famine victims, these efforts were hindered by the government's policy of blocking food deliveries from regions it considered politically hostile.

By the mid- to late 1980s, opposition to the Mengistu regime began to intensify, especially among leftist intellectuals, students, and workers. Representatives of various rebel groups soon united to form the Ethiopian People's Revolutionary Democratic Front (EPRDF). The EPRDF called for the removal of Mengistu and the establishment of a democratic government in Addis Ababa, then stepped up the armed struggle against Mengistu's forces in the late 1980s.

In 1989–90, the breakup of the Soviet Union resulted in the collapse of Ethiopia's overseas support network. Sources of much-needed economic aid could no longer be counted upon. After rebel troops began closing in on Addis Ababa in May 1991, Mengistu fled to Zimbabwe and left his government to collapse. On May 28, 1991, the EPRDF took control of the capital and declared Meles Zenawi the country's new interim president.

A NEW BEGINNING

Once in power, Meles and his backers announced their support for a federal form of government in order to accommodate the needs of Ethiopia's many ethnic groups. The government organized local and regional elections in 1992–93 and accepted the coming of independence to Eritrea. In December 1994, the government began a massive trial involving 3,000 former officials of the Mengistu regime. Charges brought against these officials— including former leader Mengistu himself (in absentia)—included murder and genocide. Ethiopian officials hope that by staging this trial they can learn from the mistakes of their predecessors.

Above: **Despite the persistent ethnic tensions and economic vulnerability of their country, Ethiopians approach the 21st century entertaining new hopes of democracy and development.**

Opposite: **The government's use of famine as a weapon in 1985 caused untold misery among millions of Ethiopians, as did its efforts to forcibly resettle rural communities.**

27

GOVERNMENT

THE ETHIOPIAN GOVERNMENT underwent a major transition during the early 1990s. Following the overthrow of Mengistu Haile Mariam's military government in 1991, the Ethiopian People's Revolutionary Democratic Front (EPRDF) formed a provisional government led by its chairman, Meles Zenawi. The new EPRDF government announced its intention to serve until the holding of democratic elections, which were eventually scheduled for early 1995. In the meantime, the government drafted a charter guaranteeing freedom of association and expression and recognizing the principle of self-determination for Ethiopia's different ethnic groups.

Meles Zenawi served as Ethiopia's president during the transitional phase (1991–1995) and shared executive power with Prime Minister Tamirat Layne. An 87-member Council of Representatives formed the legislative wing of the provisional government. This Council, established in mid-1991, included members of many political organizations and freedom movements, but was dominated by the EPRDF. In November 1991, the government created 14 self-governing regions in Ethiopia in order to decentralize power away from Addis Ababa, the capital. Most of the new regions were organized on the basis of language and ethnicity. Just how much autonomy the regional governments should have in relation to the central government is a question that has generated heated debate.

Opposite: **Women veterans at a May Day parade.**

Below: **A mural at Addis Ababa University promoting African unity depicts the leaders of the African nations.**

DRAFTING A NEW CONSTITUTION

The June 1994 poll was Ethiopia's first democratic election since the era of Haile Selassie.

In June 1994, elections were held for a 548-member constituent assembly to ratify a new Ethiopian constitution. Two key issues divided candidates vying for seats in the constituent assembly: whether the constitution should enshrine the right of ethnic self-determination, and the proper degree of state participation in the economy. Members of the Amharic ethnic group tended to voice support for a strong central government, while members of the EPRDF favored strong regional governments.

The June 1994 elections proceeded relatively smoothly. Some opposition groups, such as the Coalition of Alternative Forces for Peace and Democracy in Ethiopia (CAFPDE), boycotted the election because they feared that the new constitution would fan the flames of ethnic separatism. But despite such opposition, the polling went ahead. More than 1,400 candidates, including 42 women, vied for seats in the assembly. Of the nation's 22 million eligible voters, more than 15 million registered to vote, of whom approximately 90 percent cast ballots. The final vote count gave the governing EPRDF 484 of the 548 seats in the new constituent assembly.

President Meles opened the newly elected constituent assembly on October 28, 1994. The delegates began ratifying constitutional provisions that would give the ethnically based regions maximum autonomy, while reserving constitutional issues, defense, and foreign affairs for the central government. Some watched the proceedings of the constituent assembly with alarm. In December 1994, the opposition group CAFPDE held a conference in Addis Ababa to protest the principles behind the new constitution. Not only opposed to the document's guarantees regarding ethnic self-determination, CAFPDE also criticized provisions that identified the state as the sole owner of land in Ethiopia. But the constitution was ratified on December 8, 1994, despite protests from CAFPDE.

Following ratification of the constitution, Ethiopia held multi-party elections on May 7, 1995. The ruling party, the EPRDF, won 90 percent of the vote. The newly elected government under Meles Zenawi took office on August 21, 1995, thus ending the four-year transitional period.

POLITICAL ORGANIZATIONS AND PARTIES

The EPRDF dominates Ethiopian political life. Established in 1989 by the Tigray People's Liberation Front (TPLF), the EPRDF was originally an alliance of insurgent organizations seeking regional autonomy for the country's many ethnic groups. It defeated the Mengistu regime in 1991 after years of armed struggle. Although the TPLF is the dominant organization within the governing EPRDF, two other organizations form part of the coalition: the Tigray-based Amhara National Democratic Movement and the Shewa-based Oromo People's Democratic Organization. Meles Zenawi has led the EPRDF since its formation.

Upon final ratification of the new constitution, Ethiopia's official name became the Federal Democratic Republic of Ethiopia.

A meeting of the Women's Alliance.

Twenty-five other groups besides the EPRDF were represented in Ethiopia's Council of Representatives, which served as the country's legislative wing between 1991 and 1995.

More than 100 other political parties exist in Ethiopia, most of which are organized on an ethnic basis. During the transitional era (1991–1995), no one group was strong enough to threaten EPRDF rule. Some opposition leaders have felt marginalized ever since the June 1994 election boycotts. In September 1994, President Meles called on the boycotters to rejoin the political process, but whether the opposition groups will fully heed Meles' calls remains unclear.

Perhaps the most influential opposition party is CAFPDE, founded in 1993 and led by Dr. Beyene Petros. It played a leading role in organizing the election boycott during the voting for the constituent assembly. Like CAFPDE, the Coalition of Ethiopian Democratic Forces opposes the government's plan to devolve power and favors the creation of a strong central government to preserve Ethiopian unity. The Oromo Liberation Front seeks self-determination for the Oromo people, and withdrew from

HUMAN RIGHTS CONCERNS

Both international observers and Ethiopians themselves have expressed concerns over the Ethiopian government's human rights record in the 1990s. Two areas in particular have caused concern: curbs on press freedoms and the intimidation of government opponents.

In addition to a state-run radio service, Ethiopia has an official information bureau that publishes several newspapers. Independent newspapers do exist, but they are few and far between. Critics charge the Ethiopian government with attempting to control the flow of information in the country. In 1992, the EPRDF passed a law enabling it to detain dissenting journalists—a law it used in late 1993. During his visit to Ethiopia in September 1994, former U.S. President Jimmy Carter joined the chorus of voices expressing concern over the government's treatment of the opposition press.

The Ethiopian Human Rights Council was established in 1992 to monitor the government's human rights record. It has publicly criticized the authorities for detaining individuals without charge, dismissing government employees for political reasons, and for causing the "disappearance" of government opponents. Overseas diplomats have expressed concern over the government's willingness to arrest suspected opponents as well.

Clearly the state-run media and security services keep a close eye on opposition movements. Although the EPRDF allowed a major anti-government conference to take place in Addis Ababa in December 1993, it arrested some of the participants, thus generating international criticism.

In June 1994, the president of the All Amhara People's Organization, Professor Asrat Woldeyes, was sentenced to two years imprisonment for his political activities. Asrat Woldeyes' trial and eventual conviction led his supporters to stage several anti-government demonstrations in Addis Ababa. Many of the protesters were arrested.

In January 1993 Ethiopian security forces broke up a student demonstration at Addis Ababa University protesting U.N. involvement in the Eritrean independence process. At least one student was killed and more than 30 were seriously injured.

the transitional government in mid-1992 because it viewed the EPRDF as failing to devolve power fast enough. The Western Somali Liberation Front, established in 1975 and based in Somalia, seeks to incorporate the Ogaden region into Somalia. Its guerilla force of approximately 3,000 continues to pose a threat to Ethiopia's southeastern border.

FOREIGN AFFAIRS AND DEFENSE

Ethiopia maintains formal diplomatic relations with approximately 70 countries, including 30 African nations. The EPRDF government has recently stepped up its peacekeeping efforts in east and central Africa. In 1993, President Meles led an OAU-sponsored effort to broker a peace agreement between the warring factions in Somalia. In 1994, Ethiopia contributed troops to the United Nations force in Rwanda. Ethiopia's relations with Eritrea have remained cordial, partly because the Eritrean government gives Ethiopia access to the port and oil refinery at Assab. The EPRDF government has also established good relations with the United States and several European nations, despite lingering human rights concerns. In August 1994, Meles paid an official visit to the United States

Soldiers participate in a military parade during the Mengistu era.

and met with President Bill Clinton at the White House. It was the first such visit by an Ethiopian head of state since the era of Haile Selassie.

Ethiopia's military has been dominated by former members of the EPRDF rebel group since 1991. In late 1993, the Ethiopia government announced plans to create a "multi-ethnic defense force." That year Ethiopian troop strength was estimated at 100,000. The country's military budget currently constitutes approximately 10 percent of total government expenditure, a figure lower than the pre-1991 level.

Ethnic Somalis in southeastern Ethiopia are still fighting for independence and continue to receive assistance from a Somali-backed guerilla force.

RECENT EVENTS SUMMARY

• **Oromo armed activity.** Following the 1994 elections, the Oromo Liberation Front (OLF) began waging sporadic guerilla attacks against government troops based in the Oromo region. Western diplomats and former U.S. President Carter attempted to smooth out differences between the OLF and the EPRDF government, but differences remain, particularly over the composition and control of the Ethiopian armed forces.

• **Signs of Islamic dissatisfaction.** In November 1994, thousands of Ethiopian Muslims held a major demonstration in Addis Ababa expressing discontent with the country's secular rulers. The demonstrators called upon the government to give wider power to Islamic (Sharia) courts, grant subsidies to Islamic institutions, and guarantee equal rights for Muslims in the political, social, and economic affairs of Ethiopia.

• **Threat of famine averted.** More than six million Ethiopians were at risk of starvation in 1993–94 as another in the country's series of droughts threatened to cause widespread famine. Starvation had already claimed 5,000 victims by mid-1994. Fortunately, good rains in July and August 1994 greatly improved Ethiopia's short-term agricultural prospects and averted the threat of a major humanitarian crisis.

ECONOMY

ETHIOPIA IS ONE OF THE WORLD'S POOREST countries. Even in Africa, a continent known for its poverty, Ethiopia stands out. Its per capita income in the early 1990s was $130, second lowest in Africa next to Mozambique. Ethiopia's gross domestic product, however, is higher than average for sub-Saharan Africa: $6.9 billion in the early 1990s.

The Ethiopian economy features a mixture of state control and private enterprise. The Mengistu regime greatly extended state control over the economy in the mid- to late 1970s, but the transitional government that took power in 1991 began loosening many of these controls. Shortly after toppling Mengistu, the EPRDF announced plans to sell most state-run businesses and industries. In early 1995, the government announced its intention to sell a variety of state-run enterprises such as hotels, restaurants, small shops, and food and beverage processing plants. Officials have also pledged to return residential property seized by the Mengistu government to its original owners.

Economic performance has generally improved since 1991. Export earnings have risen, although the country continues to suffer from a serious shortage of skilled labor— a problem aggravated by the exodus of political refugees in recent years. And food shortages are still a threat due to irregular rains and inadequate harvests. Until Ethiopia's agricultural sector can be made more productive, reliance on food imports will probably continue.

Unemployment has been a persistent problem in Ethiopia, particularly in urban areas. In 1993, the unemployment rate was approximately 30 percent. *Opposite*: **A tailor at work.** *Below*: **A hardware store in Harer.**

An Ethiopian farming in the southwest. Agriculture is hindered by the lack of modern technology.

Coffee now accounts for more than 50 percent of Ethiopia's export earnings. The country's other major exports are hides and skins, livestock, and gold.

AGRICULTURE

Agriculture is by far the most important sector of the Ethiopian economy. In 1990, it constituted more than 40 percent of the country's gross domestic product and more than 90 percent of foreign exchange earnings. At least 80 percent of Ethiopia's people make a living by cultivating crops or raising livestock. The country's transportation and manufacturing sectors rely heavily on agricultural output as well.

Most of Ethiopia's arable land is farmed by peasant families using only the most basic implements. These rural dwellers tend to work on family plots and small-scale farms rather than on commercial farms. The Mengistu regime forced thousands of peasants onto collective farms in the 1970s and 1980s, but this policy has since been abandoned by the EPRDF government —to the great relief of most rural Ethiopians.

A number of crops are grown in Ethiopia, but none are as lucrative as the coffee bean. Coffee is the country's main cash crop and greatest foreign exchange earner. A high percentage of Ethiopian coffee is grown in the relatively well-watered southwestern portion of the country. Other

OBSTACLES FACING ETHIOPIA'S FARMERS

Unfortunately, neither domestic crop cultivation nor pastoralism has been productive enough to feed Ethiopia's growing population adequately. Food production in Ethiopia has actually fallen since the 1960s, making the country dependent on food imports. Several problems continue to hinder agricultural productivity:

Lack of agricultural technology. Few Ethiopian farmers have access to the fertilizers, improved seeds, pesticides, and machinery that are needed to increase crop yields. Instead of tractors and engine-driven plows, for example, most Ethiopians have only hoes, sickles, machetes, and wooden plows to use on their land.

Population pressures. Population growth has led to overcrowding, overgrazing, and soil erosion in many drought-prone areas, making farming a difficult and risky undertaking.

Irregular rainfall. Unpredictable precipitation can threaten even those farmers living outside of Ethiopia's most arid regions. Since farming underpins the Ethiopian economy, droughts can cause major humanitarian crises and put the lives of millions of Ethiopians at risk.

products grown by Ethiopian farmers include grains such as teff (indigenous to Ethiopia), wheat, barley, corn, sorghum, and millet. The most common vegetables are chickpeas, lentils, haricot beans, cabbage, onions, and lettuce. Seeds, spices, tobacco, citrus fruit, and bananas are also cultivated.

Ethiopia is estimated to have the largest population of livestock on the African continent. The most common animals herded are sheep, goats, and cattle. Ethiopia is not only home to the largest cattle population in Africa, but it is among the top 10 cattle-producing countries in the world. Cattle have proven useful during Ethiopia's periodic droughts and furnish an array of goods for export. In fact, hides, skins, and leather goods are Ethiopia's second largest export after coffee.

In November 1994, the U.N. Children's Fund announced a grant of $117 million for rural health programs and the construction of water and sanitation facilities in Ethiopia.

Ethiopia's major imports include machinery and equipment, petroleum, pharmaceutical products, and consumer goods. Its chief trading partners are Germany, Italy, Japan, and the United States.

A cotton textile factory at Bahir Dar.

MANUFACTURING

Manufacturing contributed just over five percent of Ethiopia's gross domestic product in the early 1990s. Most manufacturing plants are concentrated in Addis Ababa and Dire Dawa and produce goods for the domestic market. Food and beverage processing and textiles dominate the country's manufacturing industry; other manufactured goods include shoes, wood products, steel, cement, clothing, and leather goods. Many new enterprises have sprung up since the mid-1980s, often with help of overseas funding. Recently established industrial concerns include a cement factory in Mugher; a textile factory in Kombolcha; a tractor factory in Nazret; breweries in Harer and Bedele; and a food oil plant in Bahir Dar.

The Ethiopian manufacturing industry has been plagued by a number of problems in the past, particularly shortages of foreign exchange, new investment, raw materials, and spare parts. But since taking power in 1991, the transitional government has attempted to remedy some of these problems. It has loosened investment regulations in an effort to attract foreign capital and has offered new tax incentives to potential investors. That 400 new projects were approved in 1992–93 alone testifies to the government's initial success.

MINING

At the present time, mining is of only peripheral importance to the Ethiopian economy, contributing less than one percent toward GDP. Gold is the only mineral mined on a large scale, but the

country is known to contain deposits of platinum, salt, limestone, clay, copper, nickel, and iron. Several key mineral discoveries have been announced since the mid-1980s, including iron ore in the Welega province, coal in Kefa, bicarbonate in Shewa, potassium in Tigray, and tantalum near Shakiso. Significant deposits of coal and oil shale were discovered in the western areas of the Illubabor region in December 1994. In order to spark interest in the Ethiopian mining sector, government officials have announced new investment and tax incentive plans, and have visited Western capitals to lobby for investment.

ENERGY

Wood and charcoal are the primary sources of energy in Ethiopia, but oil and gas, hydroelectric power, and geothermal power also provide energy. Some gas reserves have been discovered in the Ogaden region, but Ethiopia is still forced to import a large share of its petroleum. Output from Ethiopia's geothermal power plants fell in the early 1990s, but potential sources of additional geothermal power have been discovered recently in the Rift Valley.

Ethiopia's rivers are a major source of energy. Most of the country's electric power is generated by hydroelectric technology. Key hydroelectric plants have been built on the Awash and Blue Nile rivers.

The Ethiopian government granted gold exploration rights to two North American firms in 1995, opening the door to approximately $150 million in new foreign investment.

41

Although Ethiopia's rivers are not generally navigable, cargo-carrying boats do ply the waters of Lake Tana and a few Rift Valley lakes. Boats constructed of reeds for travel on Lake Tana are known as *tankwas* ("TAHN-kwahs").

TRANSPORTATION

Ethiopia's mountainous terrain has made reaching remote areas notoriously difficult, and has led to the widespread use of pack animals for transporting goods and people. Many of the country's paved roads are in poor condition due to the damage they sustained during the secessionist wars of the 1980s. The country's main road—linking Addis Ababa to Assab on the Eritrean coast—is greatly in need of repair. Ethiopian officials are committed to repairing the damage to the country's roads, but progress has been slow. Major new funding for road building and repair was allocated in the mid-1990s.

The only working railroad in Ethiopia is the Addis to Djibouti line. Its poor condition has caused several serious accidents since the mid-1980s. Some repairs have been carried out, but much more work needs to be done to make the line safe and reliable.

Ethiopia's system of air transportation is served by international airports at Addis and Dire Dawa and several regional airports. Ethiopian Airlines has been called "one of Africa's success stories." It offers service to many African capitals, carries more cargo than any other airline on the continent, conducts its own maintenance, and manufactures its own crop duster aircraft. The national carrier purchased six new Boeing aircraft in 1989.

ENCOURAGING TOURISM

The EPRDF government has sought to revive the Ethiopian tourist industry after its dramatic slump during the Mengistu era. Besides making it easier for prospective tourists to qualify for visas, the government no longer requires visitors to stay in state-run hotels or apply for permission to travel outside of Addis Ababa. Indications are that the government strategy is working. In the early 1990s, an estimated 81,000 tourists visited Ethiopia annually, up from 75,000 just before the overthrow of Haile Selassie. A number of new hotels are under construction in the capital and other popular tourist centers.

Ethiopia has no shortage of attractions for the prospective tourist. Addis Ababa thrives with cultural diversity and contains many points of interest. The countryside beyond the capital is home to fascinating ancient ruins, such as the castles of Gondar (shown above), the rock-hewn churches of Lalibela, and the obelisks at Axum. Scenic wonders also abound. Not to be missed are the Blue Nile Gorge and the Blue Nile Falls near the town of Bahir Dar on Lake Tana. The Rift Valley lakes region is home to beaches, wildlife, and a popular hot springs resort. The Simien Mountains in the northwestern part of the country are renowned for their wildlife and scenic beauty.

Both backpackers and more urbane travelers could find a journey to Ethiopia rewarding. Accommodations range from luxury hotels in Addis Ababa to makeshift campsites in the countryside. Transportation options range from Ethiopian Airlines to horseback. Visitors can join formal, prearranged tours or embark on their own. Whatever their itinerary, travelers will soon discover why Ethiopia is known as the land of "13 Months of Sunshine."

ETHIOPIANS

ONE OF THE MOST REMARKABLE ASPECTS of Ethiopia is its cultural diversity. No single Ethiopian culture exists; rather, many different cultural, ethnic, religious, and linguistic groups exist within Ethiopia. In fact, the country is home to more than 100 different ethnic groups, the largest of which are the Oromo, Amhara, Tigray, and Somali. More than 70 different languages are spoken in the country. Ethiopia's diversity has greatly enriched the country over the centuries, but it has also led to conflict.

The Amhara group played a dominant role through much of Ethiopia's history, but resistance to Amhara power became widespread in the late 1970s. Undeterred by Mengistu's military might, ethnic secessionist movements led by Eritreans, Oromos, Tigrayans, and Somalis severely threatened Ethiopian unity. By 1991, Eritreans had won their independence, and the Ethiopian People's Revolutionary Democratic Front (EPRDF)—made up mostly of Tigrayans—toppled the Mengistu government.

Boundaries between ethnic groups are not necessarily impermeable. In Ethiopia—as in some other African countries—the character of ethnic groups can change as people mix with others of different backgrounds through trade, intermarriage, and friendship.

Opposite: **A young woman in Gondar in traditional Ethiopian dress.**

Left: **A Somali family. Ethnic tensions continue to exist in Ethiopia today, as the long-running conflict between the Ethiopian government and ethnic Somalis in the Ogaden makes clear.**

POPULATION

In 1994, almost 55 million people lived in Ethiopia. Almost 90 percent of Ethiopians live in rural areas, cultivating crops or herding livestock. The country's birthrate in 1990 was 45 per 1,000, a high figure compared to the rest of the developing world. The death rate of 15 per 1,000 is more typical of developing nations. The infant mortality rate in the early 1990s was approximately 114 per 1,000 live births. The reasons for the high infant mortality rate are many: Ethiopia's lack of health facilities, the spread of infectious diseases, poor sanitation, malnutrition, and food shortages. Despite health concerns, life expectancy in Ethiopia has been creeping upward in recent years. In the early 1990s, Ethiopian women could expect to live for approximately 53 years, men approximately 50 years.

Children under 15 made up almost 50 percent of Ethiopia's population in 1989, a consequence of the country's high birthrate.

An Oromo man sitting on the bus.

ETHNIC GROUPS

The Oromo people constitute at least 50 percent of Ethiopia's population and are the country's largest ethnic group. Ancestors of contemporary Oromo society spread out from their original homeland in the south central highlands beginning in the 16th century. Today their descendants live in central, southern, and western Ethiopia. Although the members of this ethnic group share the Oromo language, there is much diversity within the group. For example, some Oromo are pastoralists, some are plow cultivators, and others practice mixed farming. Some Oromo live in decentralized groups, while others live in communities characterized by hierarchical authority structures. Religious beliefs among the Oromo can vary as well. Some Oromo hold traditional beliefs, while other family members may practice Islam or Orthodox Christianity.

The Amhara make up approximately 30 percent of Ethiopia's population. The dominant group during centuries of imperial rule, the Amhara have continued to play a leading role in Ethiopian politics, despite their minority status. The Amhara's language, Amharic, has long been the favored means of communication in government, commerce, and education. Today Amharic shares official language status with English. Occasional

Besides being one of Ethiopia's official languages and the native tongue of the Amhara ethnic group, Amharic is the second language of an additional 20 percent of the country's population.

conflicts among the Amhara of different regions underscore the group's lack of political cohesiveness. Most Amhara belong to the Ethiopian Orthodox Church and tend farms in the Ethiopian highlands, where they cultivate teff, barley, wheat, sorghum, corn, and peas, and herd cattle, sheep, and goats.

Like the Amhara, the Tigray also farm in the highlands and tend to belong to the Ethiopian Orthodox Church. The Tigray are known for having founded the kingdom of Axum in the early centuries of the Christian era. Their descendants have lived in the area around Axum for centuries, and because of this, the soil in the region has become largely exhausted. The resulting poor harvests have led many Tigray to emigrate to other areas of the country in search of better land. Tigrayans speak Tigrinya, a Semitic language related to Amharic.

The fourth key ethnic group is the Somali. Predominantly pastoralists, the Somali are concentrated in the Ogaden, the region in the southeastern lowlands near the border with Somalia. Many Somalis are Muslims whose ancestors converted to Islam by the 12th century. The widespread adoption of Islam created tensions between Somalis and the Christian kingdom in Ethiopia, and a strained relationship between the Somalis and the government in Addis Ababa continues to this day. A Somali-based separatist movement has remained active in the Ogaden region in the 1990s.

A Tigray man. The Tigray number no more than 10 percent of Ethiopia's population.

OTHER GROUPS IN ETHIOPIA'S ETHNIC CORNUCOPIA

Sidama. The Sidama occupy a densely populated area in southwestern Ethiopia known for its fertile soil. Not surprisingly, the Sidamas' lifestyle revolves around agriculture. They grow grain crops, coffee, tobacco, and a banana-like crop known as enset; they also raise cattle, sheep, and horses. Religious observance among the Sidama can involve traditional beliefs, Christianity, or Islam.

Gurage. The Gurage reside in the southern Shewa region, just north of their Sidama neighbors. They are also agriculturalists whose religious beliefs can vary. However, unlike the Sidama, the Gurage have established a notable presence in Ethiopia's urban areas, where they engage in trade, manual labor, and other service occupations.

Afar. Sometimes referred to as the Danakil, the Afar people live in the arid countryside between the highlands and the Red Sea. They have a reputation for being hostile toward centralized authority in Addis Ababa. The Afar are mainly pastoralists.

Falasha. The Falasha—also known as the Beta Israel people— are Ethiopian Jews. Their descendants are thought to have arrived in Ethiopia before the fourth century A.D., when Christianity took root in the country. The Falashas numbered approximately 20,000 in 1989, but many emigrated to Israel in 1984 and 1991.

Peoples along the Ethiopia-Sudan border. These groups include the Nara, Kunama, Gumuz, Berta, Anuak, and Nuer. They occupy remote, lowland areas near Sudan and speak Nilo-Saharan languages, unlike the rest of Ethiopia's people. (The majority of Ethiopians speak Afro-Asiatic languages). Many of these borderland peoples are descendants of slaves held by Ethiopian and Sudanese Arabs in the 19th and early 20th centuries. Today these groups engage in cultivation, herding, and fishing. Their remote location has long kept them on the periphery of Ethiopian society. Shown above are two Bena women from southwestern Ethiopia.

SOCIAL STRATIFICATION

During the era of imperial rule, social status in Ethiopia depended on the amount of land one owned. But once the old order was overthrown and Mengistu Haile Mariam came to power, land was nationalized, so social status became more closely tied to one's political influence. Party members, government ministers, military officers, and senior civil servants became the new elite from the mid-1970s onward.

Today, Ethiopians tend to view government work, military service, religious leadership, and farming as the most desirable occupations. Forming the middle class in Ethiopia are those in the bureaucracy and the professions, many of whom have gained advanced educational training. Middle-class Ethiopians are highly urbanized and frequently marry across

During the long era of imperial rule, most government officials and landowners were Amhara, and Amharic was the country's official language.

The manager of a textile factory in Bahir Dar.

STYLES OF DRESS AND ADORNMENT

One of the most distinctive articles of clothing for rural Ethiopians is the *shamma* ("SHEH-mah"), a one-piece cotton wrap worn over the shoulders and arms. Worn by both men and women, the shamma is particularly common among the Amhara and Tigray people. This garment often features a colorful border, and is sometimes worn for ceremonial occasions among city dwellers as well as country people. In the higher mountainous regions, the shamma is useful in keeping out the cold wind.

Another traditional article of clothing is the *k'amis* ("kah-MEES"), a white cotton gown that women sometimes wear underneath the shamma. (Shown at right are two village women wearing a shamma and k'amis.) Western dress is now common in urban areas, although people may wear more traditional clothing at home.

Earrings, bracelets, necklaces, and religious emblems are popular forms of adornment in Ethiopia and are often made of beads or shells. Oromo women are known for their attractive necklaces, while Tigray women are famous for their gold jewelry. Scarves and turbans are worn by women throughout the country. Men in the rural areas often carry walking sticks—known in Ethiopia as *dulas* ("DOO-luhs")—as they roam the countryside.

ethnic boundaries. Many in this class left the country during the Mengistu era due to a mixture of fear and disenchantment. People engaged in commerce and trade—many of whom are Muslims or non-Ethiopians—have yet to enjoy the respect bestowed upon bureaucrats and professionals.

LIFESTYLE

JUST AS THERE IS NO SINGLE ETHIOPIAN CULTURE, there is no one Ethiopian lifestyle. The country's cultural diversity has created many different lifestyles that vary according to religion, ethnicity, gender, generation, and locale (rural vs. urban, highlands vs. lowlands).

One generalization that can be made about Ethiopian society is that the family is all important. It is the basic social and economic unit of the nation, regardless of region or ethnic group. Ethiopian families tend to be larger than North American families, partly because parents fear that some of their offspring will die from famine or disease. Sometimes families are nuclear, consisting only of parents and their children. Other Ethiopian families are extended, meaning that an assortment of aunts, uncles, cousins, and grandparents share the household.

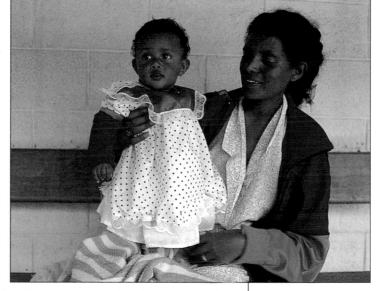

Families in Ethiopia tend to be patriarchal rather than matriarchal. Men generally head families, but women are also crucial in holding families together. The division of labor between men and women is usually well-defined, especially in rural areas. Men are expected to plant, weed, and harvest the family's crops; women, besides helping with the farm work, cook and prepare food, maintain the home, and assume primary responsibility for childcare. Although family roles are changing in some areas, elders are still treated with great respect in traditional Ethiopian society.

Opposite: **A variety of colorfully dressed people crowd the streets of Harer.**

Above: **Women are still primarily responsible for childcare in most Ethiopian families. Traditionally, Ethiopia was a highly patriarchal society.**

NAMING CHILDREN IN ETHIOPIA

Often Ethiopian children are not given names until they are several weeks old, when their character begins to show itself. Before then, parents may just use informal terms of endearment to refer to their infants. Highland societies tend to invest children's names with meaning to reflect parents' wishes or hopes. Here are some examples:

Name	Meaning	Name	Meaning
Addis	The new one	Hull Agerish	Your land is everywhere
Ageritu	The little country	Negga	It dawned
Allefnew	We made it through the bad times	Nur Addis	New life
		Sintayyehu	I have seen so much
Attalel	May s/he trick death	Tesfaye	My hope
Bayyush	If only they had seen you	Tsehay	The sun
Biyadgillign	If only he would grow up for me	Zemach	The campaigner

Some traditional societies in Ethiopia view having twins as a sign of bad luck.

BIRTH AND CHILDHOOD

Like many developing countries, Ethiopia has a high infant mortality rate, and this explains why births are sometimes greeted cautiously by parents, especially fathers. Only a minority of Ethiopian children are born in hospitals. Most are born in rural households, where elderly women often serve as midwives to assist expectant mothers. In families belonging to the Ethiopian Orthodox Church, boys are baptized on the 40th day after birth, girls on the 80th. Sometimes children are given a special baptism name that remains a secret or is used only by the immediate family. Friends and relatives are usually invited to baptism ceremonies and help mark the occasion by serving food and drink.

Ethiopian children are given responsibilities at an early age. Around the

time they reach age 5, rural children may be asked to help gather firewood or feed their family's chickens. When they are a little older, children often help guard their family's fields from intruders such as birds or baboons. Boys are eventually expected to help herd goats and cattle, while girls generally help grind grain, prepare meals, and care for younger children.

Childhood in rural Ethiopia is not all work, however. Children have ample time for play and often participate in games and recreational activities with their peers. Young people also participate fully in religious festivals, during which they can enjoy feasts, dances, music, and fellowship.

Circumcision traditionally marks the transition from childhood to adulthood for boys and girls in traditional African societies, but in Ethiopia some children are circumcised a few weeks after birth. Sometimes circumcision occurs when children are older; in Oromo society, for example, girls are not circumcised until just before marriage. Upon reaching puberty, girls from the Surma group in southwestern Ethiopia don aprons of iron beads that may weigh as much as 10 pounds. The girls keep the aprons on until marriage.

The bride and groom lead a wedding procession. Cattle are often given as bridewealth in rural Ethiopia. In some groups, the groom is also expected to give the bride a special dress as a wedding gift, often accompanied by a waistband, shawl, scarf, or shoes.

MARRIAGE

Although marital practices in Ethiopia vary according to ethnic group, one can make some generalizations. Women often marry while still in their teens, while men tend to marry in their late teens or early 20s. Marriages can occur across religious lines (between Christians and Muslims, for example), but in these cases, either the bride or the groom usually converts. Marriages rarely cross both religious and ethnic lines.

Negotiations between the bride's family and the groom's family often take place prior to the wedding and involve both male and female elders. The groom's family is usually expected to offer a gift to the bride's family, to compensate them for the loss of the woman's labor and fertility. This gift, known as bridewealth, is given in many traditional African societies to sanction marriage. In most cases, if a marriage ends in divorce, the bridewealth is returned to the groom's family.

Ethiopian weddings tend to involve an elaborate array of rituals. Some groups hold solemn engagement ceremonies prior to weddings. In one such ceremony, the groom's mother anoints her son and his best man on the forehead and knee, and then leads a procession to the bride's family home. There the bride's mother anoints the groom and the best man. In some Muslim wedding ceremonies, the groom and the best man have black markings put around their eyes and crosses painted on their foreheads. They then join a wedding procession led by elders carrying fly whisks and wearing fine clothes. Ethiopian wedding ceremonies are usually presided over by a religious official who witnesses the exchange of vows between the bride and groom.

Weddings are cause for celebration, and those in Ethiopia are no exception. Dances and chanting competitions are sometimes held after wedding ceremonies, and feasts commonly accompany weddings in the highlands. In many wedding receptions, the groomsmen will share the same table, while the bride and groom exchange mouthfuls of food in front of the assembled guests. Liquor is sometimes served to accompany the fine food. Following the celebrations, many newlyweds go on a honeymoon in which they stay in a special hut and enjoy attentive service from the groomsmen. Such honeymoons typically last one or two weeks.

A wedding meal in Lalibela.

DEATH

The customs surrounding death in Ethiopia also differ according to religion (traditional, Christian, Islamic), ethnicity, and region. In most highland societies, funerals can take several days and draw even more people than weddings. Two terms are commonly used in the highlands to refer to funeral ceremonies: *merdo* ("MUHR-doh"), which means literally "announcement of death," and *legso* ("LEHK-soh"), which refers to mourning. Christian communities often have restrictions governing proper burials. For example, such communities may refuse to give a Christian burial to a suicide victim or a person who married a Muslim. They often oppose burying Christians in the same cemeteries with Muslims as well.

Burial associations are common among Ethiopians. Besides providing members with a sense of community, these associations insure that their members will be given a proper burial. Members are expected to attend the funerals of association members and to make regular contributions to the association. Typical contributions include wood, water, grain, money, and prepared food items. Most burial associations have a leader or leaders who collect donations and enforce rules. In rural Wello society, such associations are known as the *qire* ("KEE-ray"); in some Amhara areas, the term used is *iddir* ("ID-ir").

Dying Amharas receive absolution from a priest, who also presides over the burial. A priest then leads a memorial celebration 40 days after the death.

SURMA FUNERAL RITUALS

The Surma people live in extreme southwestern Ethiopia, near the Kenyan and Sudanese borders. In the late 1980s, two photojournalists, Carol Beckwith and Angela Fisher, documented Surma cultural life in a series of vivid photographs that were eventually published in *National Geographic* and the book *African Ark*. In the course of their work, Beckwith and Fisher learned a great deal about Surma funeral rituals and captured some of these rituals on film.

In one Surma funeral observed by the photographers, the deceased person's body was wrapped in hides in preparation for burial. After milk was poured into the deceased's ears, the body was positioned in a vertical, sitting position in the grave. Participants in the funeral placed some of the deceased's possessions in the grave alongside the body. As in many Surma funerals, an elder told the story of the deceased's life through a series of chants. Later others in the ceremony sounded horns made of animal tusks.

RURAL LIVING

Approximately 90 percent of Ethiopians make their living from the land. After the imperial government was toppled in 1974, private land ownership was abolished. The nobility and landowners who had controlled so much property were forced to surrender their privileges to the new regime. The land redistribution program mandated by the Mengistu regime involved forcing thousands of peasants onto collective farms. Private property rights were reinstated by the new transitional government in the early 1990s, and the mandatory collective farming schemes have been discontinued.

Housing styles in the Ethiopian countryside vary by region and ethnic group. Cooking is done in a fireplace in the middle of the house. Sometimes families reserve a corner of their home for a few of their domesticated animals. Although villages can be found throughout Ethiopia, more common are smaller clusters of two to four homes surrounded by fields and gardens.

Nomadic Ethiopians—most of whom live in the arid lowland regions—often live in portable homes constructed of branches, grass, and animal skins. These homes are easily disassembled and transported on the backs of camels as the nomads travel the plains looking for new grasslands and sources of water. Northern rural dwellers sometimes live in houses made of stone.

Many rural dwellers live in one-room houses made of wood, straw, and clay, with wooden, grass, or tin roofs. Furniture is usually limited to a table, stools, and beds made of wood or animal skins.

URBAN LIVING

Housing in Ethiopia's cities reflects patterns of social inequality and thus varies a great deal. Some high government officials and prosperous business people live in spacious homes with appliances, telephones, and several cars. Members of the urban underclass, on the other hand, are sometimes forced by economic circumstance to live in small tin shacks without running water or electricity. Urban poverty has been a serious problem in Addis Ababa recently.

Urbanization has begun to alter traditional family structures and social roles in Ethiopia in recent years. Whereas rural women tend to be tied to household tasks, women in urban areas have more opportunities to work outside the home in schools, businesses, hotels, and restaurants, for example. The urban environment has also affected young people's lives. Because the demand for housing and well-paying jobs in Addis Ababa often exceeds the supply, many young adults have felt obligated to postpone marriage until they achieve economic security and independence. This often takes longer in the city than it does in the countryside.

Although living in Addis Ababa brings with it many opportunities, shortages of kerosene, sugar, and salt have made life difficult in recent years.

Women spinning in Tigray province.

ETHIOPIAN WOMEN

Women have traditionally been relegated to a subordinate status in Ethiopian society. They have faced persistent discrimination and have had fewer opportunities for education and employment outside of the home. However, as Ethiopia has changed, so too has the role of women.

In the rural areas, women are expected to be wives and mothers first and foremost. Women's tasks typically include raising children, maintaining the household, grinding corn, carrying loads, washing clothing, and helping with the farm work. Hard physical labor is something that most rural women take for granted. Cooking in particular takes up a large chunk of women's time. But women's roles began to change somewhat in the 1970s and 1980s, as Ethiopia's wars took many men away from their homesteads. Women were left to do the bulk of the farming, support the family, and care for the children and older relatives on their own. Many women thus became head of their households and emerged from this era with new responsibilities and a heightened sense of independence.

Ethiopian Women

Urban Ethiopian women usually have more opportunities for education, healthcare, and employment than their rural counterparts. Women in cities and towns have typically worked in the service sector, in establishments such as hotels and restaurants. Other employment opportunities for urban women include factory work and sales. A survey undertaken in Addis Ababa in the mid-1970s demonstrated that female factory workers earned only about 25 percent of the wages paid to men for the same work. But despite this history of discrimination, many women see cities as offering them a way of gaining economic independence. Some flee the rural areas in order to escape arranged or unhappy marriages; they quickly find work in Addis Ababa as waitresses or domestic servants.

Although the Mengistu government was not known for appointing large numbers of women to high office, it did improve educational opportunities for women. During the 1970s and 1980s, women's literacy rates increased significantly.

A young woman works in a shop.

ETHIOPIANS ABROAD

Between 1974 and 1991, approximately 3.5 million Ethiopians left their country in search of a better life. Twenty thousand people fled immediately after the fall of the Mengistu regime in mid-1991. Many of those who fled during the Mengistu era did so to escape violence and political persecution; others left because of religious or ethnic discrimination. Some emigrants left in search of better economic opportunities.

Neighboring countries in East Africa and the Horn absorbed many of the Ethiopians. In the mid-1980s, thousands of Ethiopians fled into Sudan, Djibouti, and Somalia to escape warfare. By 1988, over half a million Ethiopian refugees were living in Sudan alone. This mass exodus of Ethiopians resulted in a serious humanitarian crisis, as the refugees' need for food, shelter, and medical supplies far outstripped Sudan's ability to provide.

Many Ethiopians settled in the United States during this same period. Although some sought U.S. citizenship, many still actively monitored the political situation back home, sometimes staging meetings and marches or publishing newsletters relating to current events in Ethiopia. The struggle for Ethiopians living in the United States has been to adjust to a new culture without losing touch with their Ethiopian heritage. Sizable communities of Ethiopian expatriates now exist in metropolitan areas such as Washington, D.C., and the San Francisco Bay area.

SCHOOLS AND STUDENTS

Improving educational opportunities for a large and dispersed population has been one of modern Ethiopia's major challenges. In 1974, the literacy rate in Ethiopia was less than 10 percent. The Mengistu regime undertook a massive literacy campaign beginning in the late 1970s and claimed that the country's literacy rate had increased to 63 percent by 1984. Although this was probably an inflated figure, strides were undoubtedly made. In 1990, UNESCO estimated that the literacy rate among Ethiopian adults was 56.4 percent, higher than in African countries such as Burkina Faso, Gambia, and Somalia, but lower than in Tanzania and Zaire.

In 1992, 22% of children in the relevant age group were enrolled in primary schools (26% of boys and 18% of girls). For secondary schools enrollment was 11% (11% of boys and 10% of girls). Urban schools tend to be more numerous and better equipped than rural ones, which are often relatively inaccessible due to the country's underdeveloped transportation network. Rural schools have long suffered from poor facilities and teacher shortages as well. Because many rural families are traditionally reluctant

A preschool in Addis Ababa. Children start primary school at 7 years. Education in Ethiopia is free; it is hoped that primary education can soon be made compulsory, when enough schools have been built.

to send their daughters to school, students in the countryside are predominantly male. Girls growing up in the cities are more likely to attend school than their rural counterparts and can now attend university if they score well enough on national examinations.

Ethiopian schools have had to contend with serious problems of overcrowding. Class sizes in government-run schools averaged 80–120 students in the early 1990s. Some schools run two or three shifts a day to compensate for their oversized enrollments. In a typical middle school, the curriculum includes geography, history, Amharic, English, mathematics, and science. Complementing public institutions are schools run by the Ethiopian Orthodox Church. Designed for male students, these private schools stress theological training and the study of Ge'ez, the ancient Ethiopian language.

The country's premier institution of higher learning is Addis Ababa University. Established in 1950 as Haile Selassie I University, the institution was renamed by the socialist government in the mid-1970s. It has been the site of many anti-government protests in the past, both during the Haile Selassie era and after. During the Red Terror of 1976–78, protesters and dissidents affiliated with the university were harassed and killed by the

Besides regular schools, Ethiopia has technical, adult, and night schools and an array of teacher training programs. A new college for the training of civil servants opened in Addis Ababa in 1994.

Ethiopia is still lacking in school facilities, especially in rural areas.

Mengistu regime in unprecedented numbers. Today there are approximately a dozen colleges and universities in Ethiopia, but space limitations make for an extremely competitive admissions process. As it stands now, higher education is still beyond the reach of most Ethiopians.

The educational system in Ethiopia clearly faces many challenges. Because of rural economic conditions, many families have trouble finding money for their children's school supplies. They also find it difficult to spare their children when they are needed to herd livestock, work in the fields, and help with domestic chores. These socioeconomic realities have made finishing high school difficult for most rural youths. Wartime damage to schools and shortages of teachers, books, and desks only add to these problems. But with the right combination of internal political stability, economic development, and international assistance, education in Ethiopia will continue to improve.

Students reading at Axum Monastery School. The Mengistu regime closed many religious schools in the 1970s and 1980s, and brutally persecuted dissident students and intellectuals at Addis Ababa University.

EDUCATIONAL DEVELOPMENTS UNDER MENGISTU

Although the Mengistu government left a legacy of economic failure and gross human rights violations, it did undertake a major effort to improve Ethiopia's educational system. Officials were particularly interested in improving rural schools, and statistics bear this out. Between the mid-1970s and mid-1980s, for example, the number of primary schools in Ethiopia more than doubled, as did the primary school enrollment. Both the number of secondary schools and the number of teachers employed increased in this period as well. By the mid-1980s, just over 40 percent of primary school age children were actually enrolled in school; the enrollment figure for seventh and eighth grade was just over five percent. Modest-sounding figures, perhaps, but clear improvements.

The Mengistu government's close relationship with the Soviet Union, East Germany, and Cuba partly explains the educational advancements of this era. These nations funneled aid into Ethiopia and provided the country with scholarships, education specialists, and additional teachers.

RELIGION

ETHIOPIA IS HOME TO THREE of the major world religions: Christianity, Islam, and Judaism. Approximately half of all Ethiopians are Christians, most of whom belong to the Ethiopian Orthodox Church. Muslims probably constitute 40–45 percent of Ethiopians today. Relations between Ethiopian Christians and Muslims have been uneasy in the past and have at times degenerated into outright warfare. The bulk of the country's Jews, known as the Beta Israel or Falasha people, left Ethiopia in the 1980s and 1990s, but a handful still remain and preserve their ancient heritage. Ethiopia is also home to people holding traditional beliefs that vary from ethnic group to ethnic group. Those adhering solely to such beliefs probably number no more than five to 15 percent of the population.

Ethiopia's diverse religious tapestry has left a great legacy of art and architecture. Religious groups and organizations also play a vital role in Ethiopia's festivals, music, education, and cultural life.

Besides operating thousands of parishes nationwide, the Ethiopian Orthodox Church administers 12 relief centers and over 1,100 schools.

Opposite: **An Ethiopian Orthodox priest during a ceremony.**

Left· **Ancient religious structures and paintings in Gondar, Axum, and Lalibela attract visitors from all over the world. Shown here is the facade of a Gondar church.**

CHRISTIANITY

The overwhelming majority of Ethiopia's Christians belong to the Ethiopian Orthodox Church, which enjoys the allegiance of approximately 40 percent of the country's people. The most recent figures put the Ethiopian Orthodox Church's membership at more than 22 million, among whom the Amhara and Tigray ethnic groups are particularly well represented. Today the Church runs at least 20,000 parishes and employs about 290,000 clergy.

The roots of the Ethiopian Orthodox Church stretch back to ancient times. It was established in the fourth century A.D., when it became the state religion of the Axumite kingdom. The Church's influence soon became intertwined with that of the Ethiopian monarchy; so much so, in fact, that it would be the official state church in Ethiopia through the era of Haile Selassie. Because the Church's traditions came directly from the Middle East, its version of Christianity differed from that spread by European missionaries in Africa later on. The Ethiopian Orthodox Church developed separately from Western Christianity, and this explains its unique traditions based on the Old rather than the New Testament.

A priest stands outside a rock cave church in Nekutoleab.

The Church's great power and influence in Ethiopian society remained intact for centuries. However, by the 1950s, some educated Amharas and Tigrayans began to question the Church's political and economic role and its many privileges. After Haile Selassie was forced from power, the Mengistu regime forcibly took over the landholdings of the Church and divested it of much of its power. The new government followed up its seizure of Church property by imprisoning many of the Church's leaders. But although the Mengistu regime altered the organization of the Church and confiscated much of its property, its actions did not weaken the beliefs of ordinary Church members.

Members of the Ethiopian Orthodox Church believe in God and an array of angels and saints. Some Church adherents blend Christian beliefs with traditional African beliefs, as is common in much of the continent. To demonstrate their faith, the laity are required to fast 165 days annually, including every Wednesday and Friday, and during Lent and Easter.

In contrast to most Christian churches in the West, Ethiopian Orthodox Churches are usually circular or octagonal in shape. Their interiors tend to be divided into three main parts. The outer ring is where most

Worshippers are usually expected to remove their shoes before entering an Ethiopian Orthodox Church. In some churches, women are not allowed to go inside at all.

71

ORGANIZATION OF THE ETHIOPIAN ORTHODOX CHURCH

The Ethiopian Orthodox Church has long been characterized by well-defined hierarchies. At the top is the *Abun* ("AH-boon"), the venerable Church patriarch whose all-encompassing leadership role is somewhat akin to the Archbishop of Canterbury in England. Originally the selection of the Abun lay with leaders of Egypt's Coptic Church, but in 1950 the decision was handed over to the Episcopal Synod in Addis Ababa. Representing Church authority on a regional basis are 32 bishops and archbishops. (Shown here is a bishop and his assistant.)

Ethiopian Orthodox clergy are divided into three main categories. Deacons become qualified to assist with religious services after having studied for four years at a church-run school. The priesthood requires three or four years of additional study, and draws heavily on Ethiopian peasants to bolster its ranks. Priests are ranked according to their scholarly experience. The most specialized clergy are known as *debtera* ("deb-ter-RAH"). Debtera have received advanced training in areas such as musical performance, poetry, fortune-telling, and language studies. Besides these categories of clergy, the Church utilizes the services of the laity.

parishioners stay during church services; it also provides space for clergy to sing hymns and perform dances. The middle ring is designed for communion and is limited to those who have fully honored Church precepts, such as the observance of fasts during designated days. The inner sanctum houses a sacred ark dedicated to the church's patron saint. This ark is retrieved by priests during religious ceremonies and is occasionally brought outside for Church processions. Only priests may enter the inner sanctum of an Ethiopian Orthodox Church.

Ethiopia is also home to more than 375,000 Catholics, of whom approximately one third adhere to the Ethiopian rite and two thirds to the Latin rite. Ethiopia's Protestant denominations include the Fellowship of Evangelical Believers, and the Lutheran, Presbyterian, and Seventh Day Adventist churches. The country also hosts branches of the Armenian Orthodox Church and the Greek Orthodox Church.

ISLAM

Practiced in Ethiopia for over 1,000 years, Islam is an all-encompassing religion that permeates the daily life of those who practice it. More than just a religion, Islam is a culture and a way of life. It developed first in Arabia in the seventh century, when the prophet Mohammed claimed to have received the word of God—known as Allah in Islam—through a series of divine revelations. These revelations were later recorded in the Koran, the Muslim holy book. Muslims the world over are required to practice Islam's five pillars of faith: 1) recitation of the *shahada*, proclaiming faith in Allah and Mohammed; 2) prayer five times daily; 3) almsgiving; 4) fasting during the month of Ramadan; and 5) making a pilgrimage to Mecca, the holiest city in the Muslim world.

Islam first spread to Ethiopia from the Arabian peninsula in the seventh century. Itinerant Muslim clerics from Arabia introduced their religion to the peoples along the coast first and then spread farther inland. Rather than embarking on wars of conquest against indigenous cultures, these clerics initially spread their faith by encouraging Ethiopians to adapt Islam to their way of life. The strategy seemed to bear fruit. By the 10th century, Islam was being adopted by the Afar people of the Denakil region. Eventually the ancient city of Harer became the center

Reading the Koran. Muslims are found both in urban areas and in the countryside, but one contemporary observer has noted that the five pillars of Islam tend to be practiced more systematically in the cities.

73

of Islamic culture in Ethiopia. Now home to 90 mosques and shrines, Harer was used as a base from which the Muslims waged a series of holy wars against the Christian monarchy in the Ethiopian highlands.

Relations between Ethiopia's imperial rulers and the region's Muslim population varied from outright warfare to mutual coexistence. Haile Selassie's government allowed Islamic courts to operate but discouraged the formation of Islamic schools. It did little to promote the teaching of Arabic, the religion's main language. When the Mengistu regime took power in the mid-1970s, it declared some Muslim holy days to be national holidays in an effort to equalize Ethiopia's religious institutions.

The most highly Islamicized population in Ethiopia today is the Somali

"Of the two ways, that which is right; of the two decisions, that which is good— may just God lead you to follow."

—A prayer used by Somali Muslims

Islamic religious services are held in mosques and are usually attended by men only. Muslim women typically pray at home.

PILGRIMAGE TO THE TOMB OF SHEIKH HUSSEIN

Twice a year, thousands of Oromos converge at a site in the eastern foothills of the Bale Mountains to honor the 13th-century Muslim saint Sheikh Hussein. The first pilgrimage occurs in February-March to commemorate Sheikh Hussein's death; the second occurs in August-September to celebrate the anniversary of the Prophet Mohammed's birth. Each lasts approximately two weeks. Of the approximately 50,000 Oromos who participate in each pilgrimage, some will make the journey only once in their lives; others will return again and again.

Sheikh Hussein was an Islamic missionary from the Red Sea Coast who spread Islam in the Ethiopian interior in the 13th century and won many converts and even more admirers. To keep the memory of Sheikh Hussein alive, his followers built a shrine in his honor in a town that still bears his name. Originally only Muslims made the pilgrimage to Sheikh Hussein's tomb in the years following his death. But as the saint's teachings became more widely known over the centuries, other Oromos who had not yet been converted to Islam began to join the pilgrimage. Those Oromos who undertake the pilgrimage today tend to blend Islam with traditional beliefs. Some of the pilgrims are devout Muslims, while others possess only a nominal faith.

Pilgrims come from all over the country to participate in the sacred journey, some coming from hundreds of miles away. Many people proceed to the shrine on foot; others ride mules, donkeys, or horses. During the journey—which can sometimes take months to complete—pilgrims are not allowed to cut their hair or sleep indoors. They traditionally carry forked walking sticks known as *Oule Sheikh Hussein* ("OO-lay shake hoo-SANE") as they make their way to the holy site.

Once they arrive at the shrine, the pilgrims take their turn entering Sheikh Hussein's tomb by crawling through a small doorway. What follows is an experience filled with mysticism and spiritual power: "The dark, still air of the tomb is charged with the body heat of the devotees who crowd in. Some circle the floor, praying, crying, chanting. Others, seemingly consumed by a transcendental passion, writhe and throw themselves about. Others, still half concealed in corners, in nooks and crannies, sit slumped, spellbound and oblivious. . . " (Graham Hancock, *African Ark*)

While believers file inside the tomb, others remain outside to recite poetry, dance, and pray together. All of them hope that by visiting Sheikh Hussein's shrine, they will have both honored the memory of a great man and absorbed some of his ample goodness.

ethnic group; other Muslim peoples include the Afar and the Hareri. Significant sectors of the Oromo, Sidama, and Gurage populations practice Islam as well. Like their Christian neighbors, many Ethiopian Muslims blend their traditional beliefs with the precepts of the world religion. Although the degree to which Ethiopians dilute Islam varies, their faith always revolves around the Sunni rather than the Shi'a branch of Islam.

Villagers holding traditional beliefs often enlist the aid of spirit mediums, individuals who are perceived to have special powers to communicate with spirits and departed ancestors

TRADITIONAL BELIEFS

Traditional belief systems differ from Islam and Christianity in important ways. For example, such belief systems do not revolve around sacred texts or holy books but on a set of accumulated values that has been passed down from generation to generation. Traditional belief systems also tend to incorporate a wider array of gods and spirits than either Islam or Christianity. The exact form that traditional beliefs take depends on the specific ethnic group in question.

Most people adhering to traditional beliefs have faith in a supreme god who is remote but all powerful. Spirits usually serve as intermediaries between people and the supreme god. Such spirits often take the form of natural phenomena such as mountains, water, caves, and trees. Some Ethiopians believe in protective spirits known as *adbar* ("AHD-bar") spirits, which are thought to govern the fortunes of communities. The female adbar is believed to offer protection against disease, poverty, and general misfortune, while the male adbar protects against war, conflict, and poor harvests. Evil spirits exist as well. In order to protect themselves against the evil *buda* ("BOO-dah") spirit, some Ethiopians wear protective jewelry or call upon the services of a debtera or a local wizard.

ETHIOPIA'S JEWS

Unlike other nations on the African continent, Ethiopia is home to an indigenous Jewish community, known as the Beta Israel people or the Falashas. Of the handful of Falashas who remain in Ethiopia today, most live near Lake Tana and in the highlands north of Gondar. Falasha men commonly work as blacksmiths, weavers, and tanners, while Falasha women are known for their skills in making pottery and baskets. These manual trades have traditionally been looked down upon by Amhara Christians. Falashas can often be found living in the same villages as Amharas but in separate neighborhoods.

Like other Jews, the Falashas believe in one god, observe the Sabbath and most Jewish holidays, and circumcise their male children. They also follow strict laws concerning cleanliness and purity, such as that forbidding them from eating animals slaughtered by a non-Jew. The Falashas' holy book is the Torah, which is written in Ge'ez, not Hebrew. They do not use the Talmud, because this text was not codified until after the Falashas established themselves in Ethiopia.

LANGUAGE

DIVERSITY CHARACTERIZES almost every aspect of Ethiopian society. Language is no exception. With more than 70 languages spoken within its borders, Ethiopia is, like many other countries on the African continent, a source of fascination to linguists. The current official languages are Amharic and English. Other widely spoken languages include Tigrinya, Oromo, Somali, Arabic, and Italian. Given Ethiopia's linguistic complexity, the ability to speak more than one language is often a necessity. It is not surprising, then, that many Ethiopians are bilingual or multilingual.

Ethiopia's major languages belong to what linguists call the Afro-Asiatic family of languages. Afro-Asiatic languages spoken in Ethiopia are categorized into the Semitic, Cushitic, and Omotic groups. Approximately 12 Semitic languages are found in the country, including Amharic, Tigrinya, and Ge'ez (also called Ethiopic). Cushitic languages, of which there are approximately 22 in Ethiopia, include Oromo, Sidama, and Somali. Among the 18 or so Omotic languages spoken are Welayta and Kefa.

The other major language family found in Ethiopia is the Nilo-Saharan. These languages, spoken by only two percent of Ethiopia's people, include East Sudanic, Koman, Berta, and Kunama. Most of Ethiopia's Nilo-Saharan speakers live in the southwestern portion of the country near the border with Sudan.

Besides speaking their mother tongue, many Ethiopians can communicate in Amharic and a European language such as English or Italian.

Opposite: **A priest reads a prayer book.**

Below: **Presenting a Bible.**

79

AMHARIC

A music shop in Dese with a sign in English and Amharic.

A music shop in Dese with a sign in English and Amharic.

Amharic was the national language of Ethiopia during the imperial era, and has long been associated with courtly life and government. Its use by Ethiopian monarchs earned it the title *Lesane Negest*, or "language of kings." Derived from the ancient Ge'ez language in the Middle Ages, written Amharic became the official language of imperial correspondence during the reigns of Tewodros II and Yohannes IV in the 19th century. Besides being the primary language of government and commerce in the imperial era, Amharic also served as the medium of instruction in Ethiopian schools.

Amharic has a more highly developed written tradition than do most other Ethiopian languages. The Bible was first translated into Amharic in the early 19th century. Amharic writing became more widespread in the late 19th and early 20th centuries after Menelik II imported a printing press from Europe. Today Amharic is spoken as a mother tongue or a second language by approximately 50 percent of Ethiopia's population. Although no longer promoted as the language of national unity in Ethiopia, it is still considered one of the country's most important means of communication. Amharic continues to play an important role in Addis Ababa. Studies have shown that native Amharic speakers there have traditionally had more education, better literacy skills, and greater employment rates in administrative and professional positions than non-Amharic speakers.

GE'EZ

Known as the classical language of Ethiopia, Ge'ez was brought to the Horn of Africa by Semitic peoples between 2000 B.C. and the beginning of the Christian era. Written Ge'ez was derived from the Himyaritic alphabet of

A priest presents the Bible. Christian scholars translated the Bible into Ge'ez shortly after Christianity became the official religion of the Ethiopian monarchy in the fourth century A.D. Most Ge'ez literature is religious in character.

South Arabia and first appeared around the fourth century A.D. Although it was Ethiopia's most important language for centuries, spoken Ge'ez was eventually displaced by Amharic around the 16th century. In the Middle Ages, priests and monks translated Greek, Hebrew, and Arabic literary works into Ge'ez. The majority of these early texts dealt with theology, philosophy, law, and history. Perhaps the most famous Ge'ez text is entitled *Kibre Negest*, which means "glory of kings." Written in the 14th century by Tigrayan priests, it both chronicles and celebrates the reigns of early Ethiopian monarchs.

Although Ge'ez is no longer used in everyday spoken communication, it still finds a place in religious and educational settings. It is studied in some schools as a classical language, much like Latin is sometimes studied in Western schools. Ge'ez is still used by the Ethiopian Orthodox Church and is occasionally the language of choice for contemporary Ethiopian poets.

WRITING SYSTEMS

The indigenous Ethiopian languages of Ge'ez, Amharic, and Tigrinya are written using a unique set of characters derived from the ancient writing system of South Arabia. Ethiopian script contains 31 core characters that can be combined in various ways to form almost 200 more characters. Because many characters in Ethiopia's writing system represent consonant-vowel combinations and thus form syllables, Ethiopian script is said to have a syllabary rather than an alphabet. The complexity of Ethiopia's writing system makes learning to read and write more difficult than it is in English. It also makes typing rather challenging!

Other writing systems are also used in Ethiopia. The Roman alphabet is used for writing English and other European languages. Its characters can

A young mother attends a literacy class. Ethiopian script is often written using a broad pen or a fine brush. Its symbols are characterized by thick vertical strokes and thin horizontal strokes.

ETHIOPIAN PROVERBS

Proverbs capture human values in vivid and colorful ways. Sometimes proverbs convey values common to many societies throughout the world; at other times they reflect the distinct characteristics of a particular culture. The following are translations of some Amharic and Oromo proverbs commonly repeated in Ethiopia. When spoken in the original language, the proverbs often contain rhymes.

Amharic

A guest is at first like gold, then later like silver, still later like common metal.

The ear is not to be believed before the eye.

Telling a secret to a babbler is like storing teff in a bag with holes in it. (Teff is an Ethiopian grain)

He who advises evil will be destroyed by it; he who digs a hole will fall into it.

One who laughs at plowing time will cry at harvest time.

Wood will not stand up against metal nor a lie against truth.

A frog, having said, "I will become as big as an ox," blew herself up and burst.

When spiderwebs unite, they can tie up a lion.

Oromo

Indigestion is better than hunger.

If you leave those who love you, you might go to those who hate you.

He who has nobody to fear is to be feared himself.

Even if it is disagreeable, the word of an old man is never to be disdained.

One's own cottage is better than somebody else's palace.

The hawk does not fly until its wings become strong.

He who has money has relatives.

He who knows much does not speak much.

Although English is not commonly spoken as a mother tongue by Ethiopians, it is the medium of instruction in high school and university. It plays an important role in commerce, government, and international communication.

also be used to write in Ethiopian languages. In fact, Ethiopia's new government has encouraged the printing and publishing of written material in the Roman alphabet rather than the traditional Ethiopian script. Arabic script is also found in Ethiopia and is used not only for Arabic writing but occasionally for Hareri and Tigrinya as well.

THE CHALLENGES OF DIVERSITY

Ethiopia's multiplicity of languages has always made achieving national unity a challenge for the country's rulers. In the past, the imperial government sought to promote such unity by mandating that Amharic be used as the primary language in Ethiopian schools, newspapers, and on radio and television. This policy sometimes caused non-Amharic speakers to feel discriminated against. When the Mengistu regime came to power in the 1970s, it brought non-Amharic languages such as Oromo, Tigrinya, and Somali into radio broadcasts and literacy projects, but Amharic remained the language of government.

The current government is promoting the use of non-Amharic languages in keeping with its program of ethnic self-determination. The country's new administrative regions are largely organized on ethno-linguistic grounds. For example, the Tigray, Afar, Somali, and Oromo regions have declared their predominant languages to be the languages of regional government. This is the case even though their populations are not uniformly speakers of the main language. Some of the smaller regions in the southwest have opted to continue using Amharic as the language of regional government.

LANGUAGE AND EDUCATION

Though instruction in Amharic was formerly required by the imperial government, this is no longer the case in Ethiopian schools. The current government led by Meles Zenawi is seeking to introduce local languages as the means of instruction in primary schools as part of its effort to move away from Amhara dominance. Officials in Addis Ababa are also seeking to introduce English as a second language in the middle primary school years. English remains the medium of instruction in most high schools.

Introducing local languages in schools to replace Amharic has not been easy. The new policy has required an enormous effort to plan, write, print, and distribute new curricular materials for use in the classrooms. Such material is needed for all subjects in grades one through six. Those students who do not speak the predominant language of their region sometimes feel that the new language is irrelevant to their needs. The new language policy has also dramatically reduced the pool of instructors qualified to teach in each region. In most cases, only local residents can now teach in their region's schools because only they have an adequate knowledge of the provincial language.

Commenting on the confusion created by the new language policy in Ethiopian schools, one observer has written, "Change usually looks chaotic until the dust settles, and it has not yet settled in Ethiopia."

—Susan J. Hoben, Boston University

ARTS

ARTISTIC EXPRESSION IN ETHIOPIA has long been influenced by religious beliefs and practices. The Ethiopian Orthodox Church, for example, has contributed to the country's painting, architecture, and music for centuries. The icons that decorate Ethiopian illuminated manuscripts and churches of the Middle Ages are widely admired as one of the high points of Christian art. Ethiopian Muslims have a rich architectural tradition of their own. They are also known for crafting splendid pieces of ornate jewelry.

Organized religion continues to stimulate artistic expression today, but creativity in Ethiopia is not limited to churches, mosques, or sacred places. On the contrary, secular art forms thrive in the country and can be produced by both professional artists and ordinary people. Ethiopia has its share of professional writers, painters, and musicians, but many others also bring their creative impulses into everyday life. The widespread existence of oral literature, arts and crafts, and folk songs and dances attests to the continued importance of the arts in the Ethiopian countryside today. Arts and crafts popular in Ethiopia include metalwork, leatherwork, basketry, weaving, and pottery. Some craftspersons use animal horns to make crafts such as cups, shoe horns, lamps, vases, combs, and carvings.

Above: **Funerary sculptures.**

Opposite: **Uran Church at Lake Tana.**

Like most African societies, Ethiopia has many stories, folktales, and historical legends that are expressed orally rather than written down. Oral literary traditions are particularly common in southern and western Ethiopia and among the Somali ethnic group.

LITERATURE AND DRAMA

Ethiopia's oldest literary tradition is classical Ge'ez literature, the major works of which feature mostly religious and historical themes. More recent literature has dealt with village life, tensions between city and countryside, and the relationship between Christianity and traditional beliefs. Sahle Sellassie is a prominent author whose works have been translated into English. Sahle's books include *Shinega's Village: Scenes of Ethiopian Life* (1964), *Warrior King* (1974), and *Firebrands* (1979). Another well-known Ethiopian author is Berhanov Zerihun, an Amharic novelist.

Historical and religious themes have also featured prominently in Ethiopian plays. One of Ethiopia's best known dramatic works is Tsegaye Gabre-Medhin's "Oda-Oak Oracle: A Legend of Black Peoples, Told of Gods and God, of Hope and Love, and of Fear and Sacrifices." First published in English in 1965, the play dramatizes the conflict between superstition and reason in an Ethiopian setting.

A performance in Addis Ababa dramatizes Ethiopian socialist ideals.

VISUAL ARTS

Much of Ethiopia's early art was created to illustrate religious manuscripts or decorate churches. Many ancient churches seem like virtual art galleries today, filled as they are with murals, frescos, and colorful paintings depicting religious figures and symbols. Other early Ethiopian artwork was designed to pay tribute to national heroes and leaders. Artists usually painted these figures on wood, canvas, or parchment.

Commercial art began to develop in the 20th century during the reign of Haile Selassie. One popular piece of art depicts the Queen of Sheba's visit to King Solomon and is drawn in an animated, comic-strip style. Sometimes religious and commercial art can merge, as is evident by the popularity of paintings depicting St. George, an important figure in Ethiopian Orthodox circles. Artists paint representations of St. George on sheep and goat skins and then sell their works to the public. Some artists paint designs on parchment, which is then used to make lampshades.

Well-known Ethiopian artists include Afewerk Tekle, Zerihun Yetemgeta, Gebre Kristos Desta, Skunder Boghossian, and Goshu Wolde.

"Yesterday's, Today's, and Tomorrow's Africa" by Afewerk Tekle, one of Ethiopia's most celebrated artists. Afewerk Tekle's stained glass windows adorn Africa Hall in Addis Ababa.

CHALLENGES FACING WOMEN ARTISTS

Most of Ethiopia's best known women artists live in the capital, but thousands of other women contribute to the country's artistic heritage by making handicrafts in the countryside.

For centuries, Ethiopian women have been expected to be wives and mothers first and foremost and to forgo work beyond the household. Even today women's employment options outside of the home are limited. Because of the combination of family responsibilities and financial hardship, female education has been deemphasized as well. Ethiopia's social mores have thus often prevented women from competing in spheres dominated by men, such as government and business. The same is true for professional art.

Ethiopian women artists are a unique breed whose numbers are still relatively small. Many have found that the demands of raising a family leave little time for artwork. Women still make up only a small proportion of students at the School of Fine Arts in Addis Ababa, and are under-represented in national exhibitions. Some aspiring female artists apply to study overseas, but they find scholarships hard to come by.

Most of the women artists working professionally in Ethiopia today received their training at the School of Fine Arts. Some work as illustrators for newspapers, others work at the Fine Arts school or teach art in the schools.

Desta Hagos is one of the most prominent female artists working in Ethiopia today. She has displayed her paintings at a number of solo exhibitions. Trained at the School of Fine Arts in the 1960s, Desta

is best known for her paintings depicting the natural environment.

Another well known Ethiopian artist is Katsala Atenafu, the first woman to enroll at the School of Fine Arts. After graduating from the school in 1964, Katsala specialized in handicrafts, particularly weaving. She now works at the Ethiopian Handicrafts Center, which trains people to make rugs, cloth, baskets, and pottery.

The artwork produced by Ethiopian women comes in a variety of styles and genres. Many artists paint scenes of women at work baking, grinding grain, spinning cloth, or carrying firewood or heavy water jugs. In these works the hard life of Ethiopian women is unmistakable. Women artists are also known for painting portraits and nature scenes. Their works vary from realistic to abstract, somber to upbeat—no one message or style is common to all of Ethiopia's female artists. Painting is perhaps the most common art form (in watercolors and oil), but women also produce woodcuts, sketches, collages, sculpture, and tapestries. Despite considerable obstacles, women artists in Ethiopia remain determined to express themselves and to create.

Women's contributions to the craft industry are particularly notable in the production of the mesob (a basket-like food stand) and in carpet weaving and pottery.

The Ethiopian Orthodox Church is known for its intricately designed crosses made of gold, silver, bronze, brass, and wood. Handcrafted for centuries, these crosses are still used in religious services today. Those from Axum, Gondar, and Lalibela all have distinctive styles.

ARTS AND CRAFTS

A large proportion of Ethiopian metalwork springs from the country's religious traditions. Ethiopian Muslims have earned a reputation for producing lovely silverwork. Most common are decorative pieces of jewelry, such as bracelets and pins, and charm boxes. Metalwork is also prized among the Oromo ethnic group. Oromo women enjoy wearing silver necklaces on which they fasten old European coins for decoration.

Leatherwork is another thriving handicraft industry in Ethiopia, thanks to the country's ample supply of livestock. Belts, bags, and sandals are among the most common items produced and sold. The Afar people use leather to make curved sheaths for their knives; people in the Bale region are known for making fine leather saddles. The *agilgil* ("ah-GEHL-gil") is a popular handicraft that combines leatherwork with basketry. Found among highland societies, this item is a special leather-covered basket used to carry food.

Basketry thrives in many areas of Ethiopia but is particularly well-established in Harer. Skilled artisans use local grasses in making their baskets and often decorate the finished product with colorful designs. The *mesob* ("meh-SOHB") is probably the largest type of basket produced in the country; it often serves as a table in Ethiopian homes. Like baskets, woven items are also produced for domestic use and find their way into

USING THE BODY AS A CANVAS

What happens when you combine art, fashion, and tremendous creativity? Among the Surma people, the answer is body painting. Based in the mountains of southwestern Ethiopia, the Surma are a semi-nomadic people who raise cattle and grow crops for a living. Surma men are known for conducting fierce stick fighting competitions, while the women are renowned for adorning themselves with lip-plates. The Surma's rich tradition of body painting, however, may be their most fascinating custom of all.

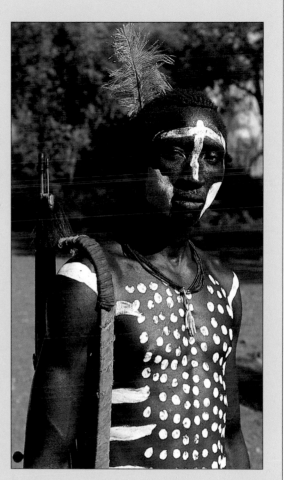

The Surma's prime body painting season comes after the October harvest, when people have sufficient leisure time to devote to their art. No one is left out; men and women, young and old are all encouraged to paint and be painted. When someone is about to be painted, their body is covered with a mixture of chalk and water. Patterns are then created by someone who removes part of the chalky mixture with their fingertips. The only limit to the designs is in the painter's imagination. Patterns can be vertical, horizontal, diagonal, circular, or any combination thereof. Some patterns are designed to attract the opposite sex, while others might be used to scare away potential enemies. Painting on the face can resemble a mask or a series of multicolored stars. Surma children have been known to paint each other as if they were twins.

The Surma are not the only Ethiopian people to use body-painting as a form of adornment. The Karo of the lower Omo River region (shown here) also paint each other. Sometimes they paint patterns to imitate the spots of the guinea fowl, or multicolored, mask-like patterns on their faces.

local markets. Heavy blankets, light cotton cloth, woolen caps, and rugs are among the most commonly woven goods. Pottery is still another of Ethiopia's handicrafts. Household goods such as jars, dishes, bowls, cooking pots, and water jugs are needed for their practical value, while flowerpots, planters, and ashtrays are produced for the tourist market.

In Karo courtship dances both male and female participants adorn themselves with decorative body paint, jewelry, and elaborate hairstyles to enhance their appeal to potential partners.

SONG AND DANCE

Ethiopian music reflects both African and Middle Eastern influences but retains a character all its own. Early music was highly religious in character. One of the first known Ethiopian composers was St. Yared, a sixth-century musician who wrote pieces for the Ethiopian Orthodox Church. Today musical chants still form an important part of church services in the Ethiopian Orthodox Church, and religious schools continue to offer training to students wishing to study church hymns, dances, and chants.

Folk music remains very much a part of life in the Ethiopian countryside. Ethiopian minstrels known locally as *azmari* ("az-MAHR-ee") help villagers mark important lifecycle events by performing at weddings, festivals, and funerals. These minstrels play traditional instruments and act as a catalyst for community participation in musical performances. Although Ethiopia's many ethnic groups have developed their own distinctive styles of song and dance, some kinds of music are common to a number of groups. Folk songs are a common vehicle for expressing political sentiments.

There are a number of musical instruments unique to Ethiopia that give folk music there its distinctive sound. Stringed instruments include two kinds of harps, the *bagana* ("beh-geh-NAH") and the *kerar* ("kuh-RAHR"), and a fiddle-like instrument known as the *masenko* ("mah-SEEN-koh"). The *meleket* ("MAH-leh-ket") is a wooden wind instrument and the *washint* ("WAH-shint") is a bamboo flute. The most common percussion instruments are the *kebero* ("KEH-beh-roh"), a rattle, and the *atamo* ("ah-TAH-moh"), a drum.

Although dance in Ethiopia varies by region, it regularly brings members of the opposite sex together for celebration and courtship. The Somalis in the Ogaden engage in special dances following the rainy season. Men wearing white robes serenade eligible women and jump high in the air to show their strength. Women in colorful gowns clap to keep time and join in the dancing to the accompaniment of drums. Karo men and women engage in a special seduction dance that often leads to marriage. Men standing in line jump in unison toward the women, who then come forward to choose their partner.

The church drum in Lalibela. Much of Ethiopia's music today still centers on religious services, festivals, and ceremonies.

LEISURE

ETHIOPIANS LIKE TO PLAY, RELAX, AND ENTERTAIN themselves, but their recreational pursuits reflect the fact that they live in an overwhelmingly rural, developing country. Many people are busy earning a living and making sure that their families are fed, clothed, and housed, and thus have relatively little time for leisure activities. The country's droughts, famines, and warfare seriously eroded people's ability to enjoy leisure time in the 1980s.

Recreational pursuits in Ethiopia do not usually require high-powered technology or expensive equipment. Sporting equipment often needs to be imported and is thus too expensive for the average Ethiopian. Given these circumstances, it is not surprising that soccer and distance running are among Ethiopia's most popular sports. Addis Ababa boasts fine athletic facilities, restaurants, movies, theaters, and parks, but most rural Ethiopians go without these things and still enjoy life.

Addis Ababa's close ties with Moscow in the 1970s and 1980s brought athletic as well as diplomatic perquisites to Ethiopia. Eager to reward the Mengistu regime for its loyal support, the Soviets donated sporting goods to the country's athletic organizations and invited Ethiopian athletes to competitions in the U.S.S.R., expenses paid.

Opposite: **Men and boys playing table football, a popular pastime throughout the country.**

Left: **Looking at the latest movies showing at an urban movie theater.**

POPULAR SPORTS

Ethiopia is considered a pioneer of African soccer. The sport was introduced to the country in the 1920s and 1930s, primarily by Italians. Ethiopians launched their first soccer club, the St. George Sports Association, in 1935 and established the Ethiopian Football Federation eight years later. After entering international competitions in the late 1940s, Ethiopia launched the African Football Confederation with Egypt and Sudan in 1956. These three nations competed in the first Africa Cup in Khartoum in 1957. Ethiopia's greatest moment came in Addis Ababa in January 1962, when its national team defeated Egypt 4-2 in overtime to win the Africa Cup. Among the thousands of adoring fans witnessing the great victory was Emperor Haile Selassie.

Today soccer is popular all over Ethiopia. National tournaments are regularly held in Addis Ababa. The capital also occasionally hosts the Africa Cup competition, which draws large crowds to the 30,000-seat Addis Ababa Stadium. International soccer matches are broadcast frequently on Ethiopian television and are very popular, especially at World Cup time.

The Olympic games have attracted many talented Ethiopian athletes, particularly distance runners. Ethiopia's past gold medal winners include

On Ethiopian soccer, The World Encyclopedia of Soccer *says this: "Before the rise of sub-Saharan soccer-playing countries in the mid-1960s, no country on the African continent was more respected for its contribution to the game's growth, and there were few who were able to match wits with the skill and determination of Ethiopian players."*

98

Abebe Bikila (marathon, 1960 and 1964), Mamo Wolde (marathon, 1968), and Miruts Yifter (5,000 meter and 10,000 meter races, 1980). The high altitude in many parts of Ethiopia provides an ideal training ground for runners, just as it does in neighboring Kenya, which has also produced world-class runners. Ethiopian athletes might have won more gold medals had it not been for the Olympic boycotts of 1976 and 1984.

In the 1992 summer games in Barcelona, Ethiopia earned three medals, placing fourth among African nations competing. Making history that year

OLYMPIC HEROES FROM THE PAST

At the beginning of the 1960 summer games in Rome, **Abebe Bikila** was a little known member of Haile Selassie's Imperial Guard. When the games were over, Abebe had become the greatest sports hero Ethiopia had ever known. His first place finish in the marathon garnered world attention because he had run the streets of Rome barefoot. Not only the first person from black Africa to win an Olympic gold medal, Abebe would be the first to win the Olympic marathon twice. He won the 1964 Olympic marathon just six weeks after his appendix was removed; his time set world and Olympic records.

Abebe's Olympic triumphs made him a hero to African sports fans all over the continent. He inspired a whole generation of Ethiopian runners, and his name became synonymous with speed and stamina. He died in 1975 at the age of 43, seven years after becoming paralyzed in a near fatal auto accident. His funeral in Addis Ababa drew thousands of fans and admirers.

Mamo Wolde won the marathon at the 1968 summer games in Mexico City, continuing where his teammate Abebe Bikila left off four years earlier. Mamo also earned a silver medal in the 10,000 meter run at Mexico City and took home a bronze in the marathon during the 1972 summer games in Munich. Despite coming in third in the marathon in 1972, Mamo's time that year was five minutes under his gold medal-winning time in the 1968 games.

Miruts Yifter won the bronze in the 10,000 meter run at the 1972 Olympics, and earned two golds in Moscow eight years later in the 5,000 and 10,000 meter races. His time in the 5,000 meter run in 1980 was the second fastest in Olympic history.

was Derartu Tulu, who won the 10,000 meter race and thus became the first Ethiopian woman to bring home a gold. Besides Derartu's gold medal, Ethiopia picked up two bronze medals in Barcelona, thanks to Fita Bayisa's third place finish in the men's 5,000 meter run and Addis Abebe's efforts in the men's 10,000 meter race.

Ethiopians also participate in basketball, volleyball, tennis, boxing, swimming, and bicycle racing, particularly in urban areas. Most of the competitors in these pastimes, however, are men. Female participation in sports is not as common in Ethiopia—or in Africa as a whole—as it is in the West. Sports have traditionally been viewed as a masculine form of recreation, whereas other leisure pursuits such as singing, visiting friends, or engaging in arts and crafts are less rigidly defined by gender.

Women smoking a pipe. Ethiopian women generally have less leisure time than men and are usually burdened with heavy childcare and housekeeping responsibilities.

SPORTS UNIQUE TO ETHIOPIA

Afar men play a game called *kwosso* ("KWOH-soh"), a kind of keep-away game in which two teams vie to keep possession of a goatskin ball. The game is very fast-paced and is played on the hard, sandy desert plain near the Denakil Depression. Sometimes as many as 200 men play at one time. Kwosso features frequent tackling and collisions. Injuries occur as players collide and attempt to strip the ball from their opponents. Contestants wear no protective padding and are usually clad only in loincloths because of the intense desert heat. Games can last an entire day.

In *feres gugs* ("FAIR-es googs"), players on opposing teams mount horses and carry lightweight wooden staffs. Those on offense try to strike the opposing players with their staffs, either by throwing the staffs or by direct contact. Those on defense ward off blows with shields made of hippo or rhino hide and dodge attacks by maneuvering their horses.

Some Ethiopian men stage war games on horseback as a form of recreation.

STICK FIGHTING COMPETITIONS

Stick fighting is one of the most popular sports among the Surma people of southwest Ethiopia. Not only does it test men's strength, coordination, and competitive zeal, but it also serves as a forum through which successful contestants can meet potential wives.

The three-month-long stick fighting "season" begins just after the rainy season and pits men from different villages against each other. Duels take place in special clearings with plenty of room for spectators. The contestants, usually unmarried males between their mid-teens and early 30s, are given six-foot-long wooden poles with which to do battle. Their goal is to knock down their opponents and remain in the game as long as possible without getting knocked down themselves. Although competitors are wrapped in protective clothing, well-placed blows often hit their mark and cause game-ending injuries. Rules prohibit combatants from killing their opponents; if this occurs, the offending contestant and his family are banished from the village.

Referees officiate in stick fighting competitions by verifying knockouts and deciding who will go on to the next round. The field of contestants gradually narrows down to two finalists who have emerged undefeated from an original field as large as 50. When a winner emerges in the championship round, he is carried on a special platform to a group of young women, one of whom will ask for his hand in marriage.

GAMES PEOPLE PLAY

Ethiopian adults enjoy games of both skill and chance. Besides cards and chess, Ethiopians play *gabata* ("geh-beh-TAH"), a board game. Similar games are played in much of the rest of the continent under different names. In this game, players place seeds in depressions on a wooden game board and then try to capture the seeds of their opponents. Potential moves are governed by complex rules. The player who captures the most seeds wins the game—and often the money that has been bet on the contest beforehand. Gabata is the Ethiopian version of wari-solo, which is possibly the world's most popular board game.

Men enjoy dancing during a break from building a house.

YOUTH RECREATION

One popular form of recreation for Ethiopian children is listening to folktales. Stories often resemble fables and feature animals as the main characters. A popular theme is the value of generosity over greed.

Children in Ethiopia have invented their own traditional games. *Debebekosh* ("deh-BEH-beh-kosh"), for example, is the Ethiopian version of hide and seek; *kelelebosh* ("keh-LEH-leh-kosh") is the Ethiopian version of jacks. Surma children enjoy participating in the snake dance, in which they squat on the ground and hold onto each other's shoulders, hopping forward and forming a snake-like pattern on the ground. As they move forward in the slithering procession, the children sing in happy voices.

Youth soccer is popular in both the cities and the countryside. Another sport popular in rural areas is known as *ganna* ("gehn-NAH") and resembles field hockey. Urban high schools tend to field teams in volleyball, soccer, gymnastics, and basketball.

School children enjoy their free time.

Boys living in Ethiopian cities sometimes raise pigeons as a form of recreation.

FESTIVALS

HOLIDAYS IN ETHIOPIA provide an array of leisure activities to people who ordinarily have little time for recreational pursuits. The festivals accompanying many Ethiopian holidays involve young and old, women and men, rich and poor, and town and countryside. Although each festival has its unique history and purpose, they all bring Ethiopians together. Feasting, visiting family and friends, giving gifts, singing and dancing, participating in parades, and playing games are just some of the activities that make Ethiopian holidays so popular.

Most Ethiopian festivals are religious in character. Many are tied to the Ethiopian Orthodox Church, which holds special services, ceremonies, and processions during the most important Church holidays. Although Christian holidays dominate the official Ethiopian calendar, other religious groups have special celebrations throughout the year as well. Ethiopian Muslims observe the holy month of Ramadan annually, during which they fast between sunup and sundown. Ethiopians holding traditional beliefs celebrate the change of seasons, harvests, and lifecycle events such as baptisms and weddings.

Above: **Celebrations in Addis Ababa marking the overthrow of the emperor.**

Opposite: **Participants in the May 1st parade.**

Whatever their religious convictions, Ethiopians observe holidays according to a unique calendar. Unlike the Gregorian calendar used in the West, the Julian calendar used in Ethiopia divides the year into 13 months. The first 12 months have 30 days each, while the 13th month has five additional days, unless it is a leap year when it has six. The first day of the Ethiopian new year falls on our September 11.

GANNA (CHRISTMAS)

Ganna ("gehn-NAH"), the Ethiopian Christmas, is celebrated annually on January 7. Church services marking the sacred day often begin as early as 3 a.m. In Addis Ababa, Ganna services are held at the Church of the Nativity and at Trinity Cathedral, where robed priests carrying prayer staffs officiate. They begin by leading hymns and then conduct Mass assisted by poets, singers, and drummers. After the service ends at approximately 9 a.m., worshippers return home to celebrate with special meals. A ball game called *ganna* is played in the late afternoon and is an essential part of the day's festivities. Resembling field hockey, ganna is played by men and older boys, who compete until nightfall. In the evenings celebrations continue as people exchange gifts and enjoy refreshments.

A festival honoring the saint Gebre Menfes Kiddus takes place annually atop a volcano outside of Addis Ababa. Gebre Menfes Kiddus established a monastery here, and to honor him, priests lead processions to the mountain with their tabots, crosses, and parasols in hand. The subsequent ceremonies draw large crowds every year.

MAJOR ETHIOPIAN HOLIDAYS *

January 7	Ganna (Christmas)
January 19	Timkat, Feast of Epiphany
March 2	Victory of Adwa commemoration
March/April	Good Friday and Easter
April 6	Ethiopian Patriots Day
May 1	Labor Day
May 28	National Day
August 21	Buhe
September 11	Enkutatash (New Year)
September 27	Maskal, Finding of the True Cross
December 28	Kullubi, Feast of St. Gabriel

* Listed according to when they fall on the Gregorian calendar

TIMKAT, FEAST OF EPIPHANY

Timkat ("TIM-keht") is the most important religious festival in Ethiopia. The holiday officially falls on January 19, two weeks after the Ethiopian Christmas, and commemorates the baptism of Jesus. Organized celebrations last three days and include processions on Timkat Eve, the commemoration of the baptism of Christ, and the Feast of St. Michael (an Ethiopian saint). Ethiopian families observe Timkat by brewing beer, baking bread, and feasting on lamb. New clothes are brought out and children are given gifts. All of this takes place beneath the clear and sunny skies of the dry season.

Formal Timkat celebrations begin with church-led processions and all-night prayer vigils. On Timkat Eve, priests remove the *tabot* ("TAH-boht," symbol of the Ark of the Covenant) from their churches and carry it in a procession, making sure that it is covered with ornate cloth at all times. The processions are led by church leaders carrying sacred relics such as Bibles,

A Timkat procession emerges from a rock-hewn church.

A feast is part of the Timkat celebrations.

Some white-robed priests chant and dance while carrying their rattles and silver-tipped staffs. They are often joined in the procession by young boys carrying bells or flags.

crosses, and silver canes. In Addis Ababa, the procession ends up at the old race course known as Jan Medha, where an all-night prayer vigil is held. At a special sunrise service the next morning, an elder of the Ethiopian Orthodox Church presides over a ceremony commemorating Christ's baptism. He dips a cross and a burning candle into some water, then sprinkles the liquid onto the crowd of worshippers. The assembled priests then carry their tabots back to their respective churches in another impressive procession.

The events occurring on Timkat day draw thousands of participants and spectators into the streets. Ceremonies and parades are held all over Ethiopia to mark the festive occasion. Shaded by bright parasols, dignitaries and church elders listen to speeches, while others read passages from the Bible before the faithful. The head of the Ethiopian Orthodox Church, the Abuna, usually attends Timkat ceremonies in Addis Ababa, wearing the colorful robes befitting his position. Church attendants carry Bibles and crosses in the outdoor procession and wear glittering, jewel-covered capes and robes of velvet and satin.

ENKUTATASH (NEW YEAR)

The Ethiopian New Year is celebrated on September 11, at the end of the rainy season. New Year's Day is called *Enkutatash* ("en-koo-TAH-tahsh"), meaning "gift of jewels," to commemorate the Queen of Sheba's return to Ethiopia after visiting King Solomon, upon which she was given precious jewelry. Today the holiday is marked by the lighting of fires on New Year's Eve. The most important celebration is held at Kostete Yohannes Church in the Gondar region. There, three days of prayers, processions, and services mark the advent of the New Year. In Addis Ababa, the biggest celebration is held at Raguel Church on Entoto Mountain. The most pious adherents of Ethiopian Orthodox tradition observe the Feast of St. John the Baptist; others simply exchange greetings or cards to mark the new year.

Buhe *("BOO-bay") is an Ethiopian holiday resembling Halloween that occurs each August 21. On that night, groups of boys go from house to house singing songs until they are given handfuls of bread to eat. In the cities, boys who perform at people's doorsteps are given money.*

Enkutatash, like many other Ethiopian holidays, is celebrated with singing and dancing.

The festival of Maskal gets it name from the yellow maskal flowers that bloom this time of year in the Ethiopian countryside.

MASKAL, FINDING OF THE TRUE CROSS

Both a secular and a religious holiday, *Maskal* ("mehs-KEHL") is held annually on September 27, two weeks after the Ethiopian New Year. The holiday celebrates the coming of spring as well as the discovery of the cross upon which Jesus was crucified. According to legend, the True Cross of Christ was found by the Roman Queen Helena in the fourth century. Later a relic of the True Cross was given to Ethiopia's kings to reward them for protecting Coptic Christians in their country. Maskal has been celebrated in Ethiopia for more than 1,600 years.

Festivities associated with Maskal today include dancing, feasting, parades, gun salutes, and the setting of bonfires. In Addis Ababa, an elaborate holiday procession goes from Africa Hall and Jubilee Palace to Maskal Square. Approximately 100,000 people come to watch the parade each year, which features bands, finely decorated floats, and the participation of priests, scouts, civic groups, soldiers, and schoolchildren. Some priests wear white turbans and robes, while others are clad in more colorful garb, including bright caps and flowing capes. Many bring with them ornate bronze crosses, sometimes mounted on poles or worn as pendants. Children participate in the parade by singing and dancing to the accompaniment of drums. At sunset, the assembled crowd watches participants throw torches onto a tall bonfire, which burns all night. This ceremony is observed not only in the capital, but in most town squares and village marketplaces throughout the country.

KULLUBI, FEAST OF ST. GABRIEL

Kullubi ("koo-LOO-bee"), one of the most popular festivals, honors St. Gabriel, a patron saint for many Orthodox Christians, who is viewed as a great protector and miracle worker. Each December 28, he is honored with special celebrations all over the country. Those eager to pay tribute make a pilgrimage to St. Gabriel's church in Kullubi, located in the Harer region 40 miles from Dire Dawa. Some of the faithful arrive by car; others find

A cow is slaughtered to feed pilgrims in Kullubi. When they arrive in Kullubi, pilgrims set up tents and cooking fires, sit down for a sip of home-brewed beer, and purchase food items from itinerant vendors. During the festival, public transportation from Addis Ababa to Kullubi can barely keep up with demand. Seats on trains, planes, and buses sell out weeks in advance.

seats on buses or trucks; still others ride mules. Many of the pilgrims walk to the site.

Eventually about 100,000 people converge on Kullubi. The pilgrims' primary goal while at Kullubi is to make vows and give thanks to St. Gabriel. Those who can, crowd into the church for Mass; those left outside listen to services broadcast over loudspeakers. Some pilgrims also bring their babies to be baptized. In fact, during the three-day celebration at Kullubi, approximately 1,000 babies are baptized, and many are named after the saint their parents have come to honor.

FOOD

TWO WORDS ARE KEY to understanding Ethiopian cuisine: hot and spicy. Many herbs and spices are used to give Ethiopian food its fiery flavor, but perhaps the most essential ingredient is *berbere* ("ber-BER-ray"), a hot pepper sauce common in many Ethiopian dishes. First-time tasters can find foods spiced with berbere truly scorching, but Ethiopians wouldn't think of having a meal without it. Berbere is a particularly important ingredient in *wat* ("weht"), a type of spicy stew that is the country's most popular dish.

Besides enjoying spicier food than most Westerners are accustomed to, Ethiopians are less prone to take food for granted. Many families struggle to put enough food on the table and are ever conscious of the specters of drought and starvation that have taken such a toll in the past. Although Ethiopia has long since recovered from the famine of 1984–85, the country still depends on food imports to feed its people.

Opposite: **Women grinding spices. Spices are an essential part of Ethiopian cuisine.**

Left: **A relief worker feeds children during a famine. Food shortages are a continuing concern because of irregular rainfall, a decline in productive agricultural land, and the fast-growing population.**

113

Cooking *injera* ("in-JAIR-ah"), Ethiopian bread. Rural women usually cook their family's meals over a fire; urban women may have a kerosene stove over which to cook. Electric ranges are found only in the wealthiest urban homes.

Most cooking is done by women. Rural women probably spend more time cooking than on any other task.

COOKING, ETHIOPIAN STYLE

Most rural Ethiopians supply their own food, either by growing grains, fruit, or vegetables or by raising chickens, goats, sheep, or cattle. Although Ethiopians in the countryside often go to market to obtain certain spices or specialty food items, they rarely have the chance to shop in large grocery stores. Such supermarkets exist only in large urban areas such as Addis Ababa. Only small numbers of Ethiopians have access to frozen and convenience foods, and relatively few own cooking appliances such as refrigerators, electric stoves, or toasters. Food preparation is much more time consuming and labor intensive in Ethiopia than it is in the West.

Meal preparation typically involves gathering wood for the cooking fire, grinding grain, pounding and mixing spices, baking, carrying water, washing and cutting vegetables, and much more. Despite the complexity of many of their dishes, Ethiopian women do not traditionally use written recipes when cooking. Instead, culinary practices are passed from one generation to the other through example and instruction.

114

POPULAR DISHES

Ethiopia's national dish is wat, a type of stew spiced with hot pepper sauce. The key to wat is its rich and spicy sauce, which usually contains salt, garlic, ginger, black pepper, cardamom, onion, lemon juice, nutmeg, wine, water, spiced butter, paprika, fenugreek seeds, and berbere. The most popular form of wat, *doro wat* ("DOR-oh weht"), contains chicken. However, wat can also contain beef, lamb, fish, or vegetables. Vegetarian wat, based on lentils, beans, or chickpeas, is eaten by members of the Orthodox Church on fast days.

The most important side dish in Ethiopian meals is injera, a special kind of bread made from teff, an Ethiopian grain. When preparing injera, Ethiopian women first hand-grind teff grain to make flour. Next they make the batter by combining the flour with water and letting the mixture ferment for three or four days. Then they pour the fermented batter in a circular pattern onto a clay griddle over a fire. Cooking only takes a few minutes. The finished product is a thin, pancake-shaped bread with little pits from fermentation bubbles. It has a mild, slightly sour taste and a spongy, limp texture. During mealtimes, injera is kept in a covered basket beside the main dish. Diners use the bread to scoop up food and absorb spicy sauces.

A traditional Ethiopian meal includes a selection of wats served on injera and accompanied by *tej* ("tehj"), a honey wine. The meal is laid out on a mesob, a traditional Ethiopian basket used as a table.

115

Alecha *("ab-LEH-chah") is a milder stew than wat. It commonly contains chicken or beef combined with onions, potatoes, carrots, cabbage, green peppers, chilies, garlic, turmeric, ginger, black pepper, and salt.*

Afar women making bread.

As a rule, Ethiopians do not consume nearly as much meat as Westerners. When a meal does call for meat, chicken, beef, or lamb are typically the most common choices; in the dry lowland regions, people sometimes eat goat or camel meat. *Kitfo* ("KIT-foh") is a popular dish made with raw chopped beef and spices. The first step in making kitfo is to sauté onions, green peppers, chilies, ginger, garlic, and cardamom in spiced butter. Once this is done, lemon juice, berbere, salt, and raw beef are added. The finished kitfo can be an appetizer or a main dish and is often served in green peppers or with injera.

Dried beef is commonly eaten in rural areas as well. The meat is cut into strips, cured with salt, pepper, and berbere, and hung out to dry in a cool place for approximately two weeks. It is then eaten as a snack food.

One of Ethiopia's most popular vegetarian meals is *yataklete kilkil* ("yah-TAH-kelt KIL-i-kil"), a casserole of fresh vegetables flavored with garlic and ginger. It is served as a main dish during Lent and as a side dish at other times of the year. Typical ingredients for yataklete kilkil besides garlic and ginger include potatoes, broccoli, carrots, green beans, onions, cauliflower, green pepper, hot chilies, salt, pepper, and scallions. This meal is traditionally served with injera or rice. *Yemiser selatta* ("yeh-mis-SIR seh-LAH-tah") is another vegetarian favorite. This is a lentil-based salad with shallots and chilies, commonly served during Lent.

Although injera is the most popular accompaniment to Ethiopian meals, a

THE SPICE OF LIFE

It would be hard to imagine Ethiopian food without spices. They are an essential ingredient of the country's most popular meal—wat—and give countless other dishes their flavor and heat. Among Ethiopia's most commonly used spices are pepper, garlic, bishop's weed, rue, mint, cloves, cinnamon, turmeric, and nutmeg.

Several of these spices are combined with powerful peppers, herbs, and water to form berbere, the favorite hot sauce of Ethiopian cooks. Berbere is a key ingredient in beef and chicken stews and is used as a dip for raw meat dishes. The exact ingredients used to make berbere form a long list: paprika, red pepper, salt, ginger, onion, garlic, cloves, cinnamon, nutmeg, cardamom, allspice, black pepper, fenugreek, coriander, red wine, water, vegetable oil, cumin, and turmeric. These items are delicately mixed and heated to form a zesty sauce as hot as fire.

The famous South African author Laurens van der Post tried berbere on one of his early trips to Ethiopia. When his hosts offered him raw meat dipped in berbere sauce, van der Post decided to be adventurous. "If one must eat meat raw," he recalled later, "it is surely best done in this way, for the sauce gives the impression of being hot enough to cook the meat right on the tongue."

number of other side dishes are commonly served throughout the country as well. *Dabo kolo* ("DAH-boh KOH-loh") is a roasted biscuit made with wheat flour, berbere, sugar, and salt. It makes a crunchy, spicy snack. *Yeshimbra assa* ("yeh-shim-BRAH AH-sa") is the name for fish-shaped snacks made from chickpea flour. Ground chickpeas, oil, onions, berbere, salt and pepper are mixed and formed into a paste. They are then molded into fish shapes, fried, and served. For dessert, Ethiopians sometimes serve strawberries; stalks of sugarcane are also chewed as sweet snacks.

A special butter is used widely as a spread and in cooking. This spicy butter, known locally as *niter kebbeh* ("NIT-er ki-BAY"), is made from butter, onions, garlic, ginger, turmeric, cardamom, cinnamon, cloves, and nutmeg. It is an essential ingredient in wat.

BEVERAGES

Ethiopian cups and glasses are usually filled with milk, beer, wine, tea, or coffee. Milk is traditionally a children's beverage and can come from camels, cows, or goats. Ethiopia's own variety of home-brewed beer is known as *tella* ("TEH-lah"), and can be made from barley, corn, or wheat. Tej, the Ethiopian wine, is made from honey and has been served in the country for centuries. It is usually poured from distinctive narrow-necked glass decanters.

Coffee has a long history in Ethiopia and is a favorite after-dinner beverage.

DINING OUT IN ADDIS ABABA

Addis Ababa's large population, international visitors, and cultural diversity feed a thriving restaurant industry. Besides traditional Ethiopian cuisine, one can find restaurants in the capital specializing in Italian, Indian, and Chinese food. Places to eat out range from streetside vendors and small snack bars to gourmet restaurants. Bakeries do a good business too. The international restaurants in the downtown area cater to the city's sizable business and official clientele. An old favorite of visitors is the Addis Ababa Restaurant, which serves traditional Ethiopian food in highly attractive surroundings.

ETHIOPIA—HOME OF THE COFFEE BEAN

The word *coffee* is believed to have been derived from Kefa, the region in southwestern Ethiopia where coffee has been grown for centuries. In fact, legend has it that Ethiopia is the original home of the coffee bean.

Ethiopians enjoy coffee as much as Westerners do, but relatively few buy their coffee in a can. More often, rural Ethiopians roast their coffee beans themselves, grind them, and then pour hot water over the grounds. If they lack sugar, Ethiopians sometimes sweeten their coffee with honey. Coffee is the perfect beverage to round out an Ethiopian meal, particularly a spicy main dish. It is also a popular drink to serve guests.

Coffee is big business in Ethiopia. It is the country's number one export and often finds its way to specialty coffee shops in the United States. Commonly exported Ethiopian coffees include the Sidamo, Yergacheffe, and Harer varieties.

TRADITIONS AND ETIQUETTE

The majority of Ethiopians living in the countryside do not have three fixed mealtimes for breakfast, lunch, and dinner. Instead, they may have one or two hot meals per day and eat smaller portions of bread or dried meat as snacks. If breakfast is eaten, items served might include bread, hard-boiled or raw eggs, or porridge. Often only injera will be eaten in the morning. Ethiopians usually eat their main meal in the evening.

Sit-down meals often start with tej (honey wine) and bread. When the main course is served, Ethiopians do not usually use forks or spoons to eat. Instead they use injera to scoop up food and absorb the sauces. Letting one's fingers touch either the main dish—such as wat—or one's mouth while eating is considered bad manners.

Injera is the "utensil" used for scooping up food. It is traditionally held in the right hand while eating.

DORO WAT (SPICY CHICKEN STEW)

Serves 4-5

Berbere mixture
$1/2$ teaspoon ground ginger
$1^1/2$ tablespoons cayenne pepper
$1/8$ teaspoon ground cloves
$1/4$ teaspoon cinnamon

Combine spices. Makes $1^1/2$ heaping tablespoons.

Doro wat
3-lb. (1.35 kg) chicken, cut into pieces
1 stick of butter
$1^1/2$ lbs. (.7 kg) onion, finely chopped
1 teaspoon chopped garlic
$1^1/2$ heaping tablespoons berbere
$4^1/2$ oz. (125 g) tomato paste
5 hard-boiled eggs, slightly scored
$1/2$ teaspoon ground black pepper

1. Remove skin from the chicken and score each piece slightly with a knife so the sauce can penetrate.

2. In a large pot, melt the butter, then sauté the onions and garlic for five minutes. Add berbere, followed by tomato paste, stirring occasionally while the mixture simmers for about 15 minutes. Stir in the chicken, a piece at a time, coating well with the sauce.

3. Continue to simmer, adding enough water to maintain the consistency of a thick soup. When chicken is half done, after about 20 minutes, put in the hard-boiled eggs. Cover and continue cooking until chicken is tender. The dish is ready when oil has risen to the top. Add black pepper and let stand for a few minutes.

4. Serve with bread, rolls, or rice. (Injera commonly accompanies doro wat in Ethiopia).

Ethiopian restaurants have opened up in many major U.S. cities, making Ethiopian food probably the most widely available type of African cuisine in the United States.

ETHIOPIA

A **B** **C** **D**

Scale 1:9,200,000

0 50 100 150 200 Miles
0 100 200 300 Kilometers

Capital city
Major town
Mountain peak

Feet	Meters
16,500	5,000
9,900	3,000
6,600	2,000
3,300	1,000
1,650	500
660	200
0	0

1

SAUDI ARABIA

ERITREA

Red Sea

**REPUBLIC
OF
YEMEN**

SUDAN

N

Axum • Adwa

Tekeze

TIGRAY

*Denakil
Depression*

Strait of Bab al-Mandah

Gulf of Aden

2

*Ras Dashan
(15,158 ft / 4,620 m)*

GONDAR *Simien
Mountains* ▲

Mekele

Gondar •

Amhara

Tana

Lalibela

WELO

DJIBOUTI

Bahir Dar •

GOJAM

*Choke
Mountains*

Dese

Abbai (Blue Nile)

Debre
• Markos

Awash

Debre
Barham

Dire Dawa

3

WELEGA

SHEWA

ADDIS ABABA

Akaki

Awash

Harer

Debre Zeyit

Nazret

Ahmar Mountains

Koka

Zwai

Baro

ILUBABOR

• Jima

*Abiata
Shala* Langano

ARUSI

HARER

Akobo

KEFA

*Ogaden
region*

*Mendepo
Mountains*

Shebelle

4

Abaya

GEMU GEFA

Adola •

BALE

SOMALIA

Shamo

SIDAMO

5

UGANDA **KENYA**

*INDIAN
OCEAN*

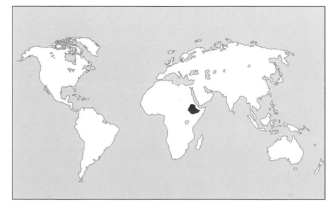

QUICK NOTES

OFFICIAL NAME
Federal Democratic Republic of Ethiopia

LAND AREA
437,600 square miles (1,133,380 square kilometers)

POPULATION
54,927,108 (July 1994 estimate)

CAPITAL
Addis Ababa

PROVINCES
Arusi, Bale, Gemu Gefa, Gojam, Gondar, Harer, Ilubabor, Kefa, Shewa, Sidamo, Tigray, Welega, Welo

NATIONAL SYMBOL
Lion

NATIONAL FLAG
Three horizontal stripes of green, yellow, and red

MAJOR RIVER
Blue Nile/Abbai River

MAJOR LAKE
Lake Tana

HIGHEST POINT
Ras Dashan peak in Simien Mountains (15,158 feet/4,620 meters)

NATIONAL/OFFICIAL LANGUAGES
Amharic (first); English (second)

MAJOR RELIGIONS
Ethiopian Orthodox (Christian), Islam, traditional beliefs

CURRENCY
Birr (5 birr = US $1)

MAIN EXPORTS
Coffee, leather goods

IMPORTANT ANNIVERSARIES
Victory at Adwa (March 2)
Downfall of the Derg (May 28)

LEADERS IN POLITICS
Haile Selassie, emperor 1930–1974
Mengistu Haile Mariam, leader of military government 1977–1991
Meles Zenawi, president 1991–present

LEADERS IN LITERATURE
Berhanov Zerihun
Sahle Sellassie
Tsegaye Gabre Medhin

IMPORTANT RELIGIOUS HOLIDAYS
Ganna (Christmas): January 7
Timkat (Epiphany): January 19
Maskal (Finding of the True Cross): September 27
Kullubi (Feast of St. Gabriel): December 28

GLOSSARY

Abun ("AH-boon")
Official head of the Ethiopian Orthodox Church.

berbere ("ber-BER-ray")
A spice mixture added to many Ethiopian dishes.

bereha ("ber-eh-HAH")
The semidesert region, including the Denakil Depression and other low-lying areas.

dega ("DEH-ga")
The cool region, chiefly the Amhara Plateau.

Derg ("durg")
The military government that ruled Ethiopia from 1974 to 1991. Came under the leadership of Lt. Col. Mengistu Haile Mariam in 1977. *Derg* literally means "committee" in Amharic.

Enkutatash ("en-koo-TAH-tahsh")
Literally "gift of jewels," the name for the Ethiopian New Year's Day.

EPRDF
Ethiopian People's Revolutionary Democratic Front. The EPRDF gained control of the Ethiopian government in 1991 under the leadership of Meles Zenawi and has remained in power ever since.

Ganna ("gehn-NAH")
Ethiopian Christmas.

injera ("in-JAIR-ah")
A flat bread made from teff flour.

k'amis (kah-MEES")
A white cotton gown that women sometimes wear underneath the *shamma.*

kolla ("KOH-la")
The hot region, including the eastern Ogaden, valleys of Blue Nile and Tekeze rivers, and areas along Kenyan and Sudanese borders.

kur ("kuhr")
The alpine region, including the highest elevations.

Merkato ("mer-KAH-toe")
The large, open-air market in Addis Ababa. Attracts Ethiopians from all over the country.

mesob ("meh-SOHB")
A large basket used as a table.

shamma ("SHEH-mah")
A one-piece cotton wrap worn over the shoulders and arms.

teff
A grain indigenous to Ethiopia.

Timkat ("TIM-keht")
Epiphany, the most important religious festival in Ethiopia.

wat ("weht")
A highly spiced stew eaten with *injera.*

weina dega ("WAY-nuh DEH-ga")
The temperate region, including the lower regions of the Amhara and Somali plateaus.

BIBLIOGRAPHY

Beckwith, Carol, and Angela Fisher. *African Ark: People and Ancient Cultures of Ethiopia and the Horn of Africa.* New York: Harry N. Abrams, 1990.

Brown, Judith R. *Farnji: A Venture into Ethiopia.* Santa Barbara: Fithian Press, 1994.

Gilkes, Patrick. *Conflict in Somalia and Ethiopia.* New York: New Discovery Books, 1994.

Kurtz, Jane. *Ethiopia: The Roof of Africa.* New York: Dillon Press, 1991.

Ofcansky, Thomas. *Ethiopia: A Country Study.* Washington, DC: U.S. Government Printing Office, 1992.

Shelemay, Kay K. *A Song of Longing: An Ethiopian Journey.* Champaign: University of Illinois Press, 1992.

Stewart, Gail B. *Ethiopia.* New York: Crestwood House, 1991.

INDEX

INDEX

INDEX

PICTURE CREDITS